A Taste of Fiction

An Appetizing Sampler of **New Zondervan Fiction**

ZONDERVAN™

GRAND RAPIDS, MICHIGAN 49530 USA

ZONDERVAN™

Requests for information should be addressed to:

Zondervan, *Grand Rapids, Michigan 49530*

Interior design by Michelle Espinoza

Printed in the United States of America

05 06 07 08 09 10 /❖ DCI/ 10 9 8 7 6 5 4 3 2 1

Contents

Foreword

Dear Fiction Fans,

Hearing from readers . . . hearing from you, is one of the most enjoyable facets of our jobs at Zondervan. The letters and emails we receive letting us know how a Zondervan fiction title impacted a life and helped strengthened someone's faith walk continually reaffirms our belief in the power of story.

An FDNY firefighter separated from his wife and children wrote, "Your book helped me remember who I am and that the only thing that matters is my family." Another reader wrote that reading Zondervan's Christian fiction makes her think about her own walk with the Lord and spurs her to keep pressing on. A pastor wrote that "each (Zondervan fiction) book and story has peeled away more and more of the layers of understanding, and deepened and enriched my faith journey."

So you can see why we are so excited about sharing with you a sampling of our upcoming fiction. In this book, you will find excerpts from wonderful new stories, be introduced to unforgettable characters, and journey with them through adventure, intrigue, faith, and love.

Sit back, relax, enjoy—and may you be blessed by the gift of story.

Karen Ball, Editor
Sue Brower, Marketing Director
Sherry Guzy, Associate Marketing Director

P.S. We love to hear from you, so be sure to let us know what you think about our fiction by emailing us at fictionclub@zondervan.com or writing to us at Zondervan, 5300 Patterson Ave. S.E., Fiction, B-22, Grand Rapids, MI 49530.

ON AIR

When Nightime Radio Becomes Daytime Danger,
Mayor Madison Glenn Must Act . . .

Before Another Dies

ALTON
GANSKY

ZONDERVAN

Alton Gansky

Alton Gansky has written a number of novels, including *The Prodigy*, *Dark Moon*, and the J.D. Stanton Mysteries series. He also writes non-fiction books that explore the mysteries of faith, the Bible, and God. He and his wife, Becky, have three adult children.

A Word From the Author

Faith isn't lived in isolation. The world continues around us; the workplace demands our attention; evil continues to wound lives. Taking faith learned in the pew and utilizing it in the place we live can be daunting, especially for those new belief. When fear and tragedy invade the life of a believer, faith in God is often all that is left—and that is more than enough. In *Before Another Dies*, Mayor Maddy Glenn faces danger and a string of tragedies that force her to relive her darkest days. Her faith is young and untried and now it must grow to meet a frightening need.

Maddy must help solve a string of murders and help a dear friend through a horrible loss—one not very different from what she experienced years before. This time, however, she has a tool she didn't have before: faith. In writing, *Before Another Dies*, the second Madison Glenn book, I explored faith on the front burner. It is easy for Christians to see faith as an "additive" to life instead of life itself. Danger, sorrow and loss can make faith the core of life, not something tied to the fringes. My hope is for readers to see real faith in real life.

Alton Gansky

Chapter 1

He was in my parking place.

And that was the least of my worries.

Last week, I began my third year as mayor of Santa Rita. Prior to that, I served two four-year terms on the city council. After eleven years in public life, I thought I had seen everything.

People are attracted to the city. Maybe it's because Santa Rita is snuggled next to the Southern California ocean. Maybe it's because our nights are warm and our days only slightly warmer. We don't do hot; and we certainly don't do cold. The ocean serves as our personal heat sink. Our restaurants are exceptional, and our ocean is blue enough to make the sky envious. People come to Santa Rita to escape Los Angeles to the south. Some just pass through on the way to Santa Barbara to the north.

As I said, people are attracted to the city. Most are reasonable, civil, and normal people, but we have our share of fringe personalities. We have transients who wander our streets content to stay as long as their restless souls will allow. We have homeless who sleep in our parks and between downtown buildings. We even have our share of social gadflies. Some who have burning messages for their civic leaders. Most are harmless; a few are scary.

Last week, Bobby "Street Dog" Benson was waiting for me when I arrived at city hall. I had chosen to park in front of the building as I usually do in the mornings. In the afternoon, I hide my car in the back lot. Fewer disruptions that way. Street Dog—he named himself—had been sent by some alien race or another to warn me of an impending invasion. The mother ship was due to land on the beach just south of the pier at precisely 3:10 that afternoon. Street Dog hears voices. I thanked him and rewarded his civic contribution with a five dollar bill I hoped he'd use to buy an Egg McMuffin. Street Dog left satisfied. The mother ship never arrived.

Yes, I've seen it all. Or at least I thought I had until, under a bright January sky, I pulled into the front lot of city hall and aimed my car toward the reserved space with the sign that read, "The Hon. Mayor Madison Glenn." That's me, except I prefer the name Maddy. Madison sounds too ... I don't know—something. My father, a history professor at the University of Santa Barbara, named me after a dead president. He likes dead presidents.

I directed my silver Lincoln Aviator up the drive and down the lot. A second later, I saw it: a lime green AMC Gremlin hatchback that appeared as if it had been traveling nonstop since the day it rolled off the assembly line sometime in the early seventies.

"Great." I'm not stuck on my title, nor do I think the citizens who elected me to be their first full-time mayor should treat me like royalty. I had moved beyond feeling that a reserved parking space made me important. The principle of the thing, however, bothered me. After all, the space was, well, reserved, and it had a sign that said so. Just like the space next to it for the city manager, city attorney, and the members of the council.

I had a choice to make. I could simply drive around to the back of the building and park there, or I could confront the space thief. Most days, I would have chosen the former. This day, I stopped my SUV a few feet from the Gremlin and waited for the driver to catch my hint. I was ready with my patented "how-dare-you" scowl.

He didn't move. I gunned the engine and let the eight cylinders roar slightly less than a polite, "Hey, buddy." Nothing. Was he asleep? The urge to honk grew but I chose a more diplomatic approach, one fitting an elected official, especially one facing an election.

I exited my car and started forward. It was still early, just seven-thirty and the sun was still crawling up the eastern sky, just beyond the coastal hills. Most of the city employees would not be around for another half hour. A brief but pungent fear rolled over me. What if the guy was off his rocker? I mean, he *was* driving a Gremlin. I considered calling security, but I was afraid I'd sound petty. A lot of things have changed in my life over the last six months, but I was still in a wrestling match with pride.

I approached the driver's side door and tapped the glass with the knuckle of my index finger. "Excuse me, sir." I tried to sound as pleasant as a woman could at seven-thirty and one cup of coffee shy of contentment. "May I help ...?"

The driver was slumped in his seat. I assumed he was snoozing, perhaps having over exercised his right to knock back cold ones at the local bar.

He wasn't asleep. Spiders crawled down my spine, and I took a step back.

Returning to my car, I pulled the cell phone from my purse and dialed a number well known to me. Ringing was replaced by a curt voice. I made myself known. "This is Maddy Glenn. I don't suppose Chief Webb is in yet." The cop who answered assured me that Webb was in but that he was in some sort of early morning meeting. "I need to speak to him right away."

"It might be better if we wait for the meeting to end. He hates interruptions. Trust me; he *really* hates to be interrupted."

"I understand. Please tell him *Mayor* Glenn needs him on the phone." There was a pause, then I was in the never-never land of hold.

"Webb." Chief Bill Webb had a gruff voice that matched his face. He sounded even crustier than usual, something I attributed to the early hour and my having yanked him out of his meeting.

"Chief Webb, it's Maddy."

"Madam Mayor." What little courtesy there was in his voice evaporated. Webb and I have history. He doesn't like me and never has. The feeling is mutual which is a bit awkward since he saved my life a few months back. I owed him a lot but he never brings it up. He was too professional. Regardless of our mutual misgivings, I know him to be an excellent police officer and superior administrator. Our problems have to do with politics and money and goals and money; and to make things worse, we've disagreed over money. He wants more; I don't want to give it.

"I'm sorry to disturb you so early, but this is important." I took a deep breath. "I just pulled into the front lot, and there is a car in my parking space—"

"You didn't just pull me out of an officer review meeting to evict some guy from your parking space, did you? Unbelievable. Call security. That's their job. Call a tow truck."

"You don't understand, the driver is in the car—"

"Tell him who you are, then tell him to beat feet."

"I would, but he's dead." Silence. I could hear people talking in the background and the chief breathing. "You there?"

"I'm here. You sure he's dead?"

I sighed. "Head tilted to one side, cloudy eyes open and unblinking, mouth agape . . . Oh, did I mention that he doesn't appear to be breathing?"

"I'll be right there." He hung up.

I closed my flip phone and forced myself to the Gremlin again. The man hadn't budged, but then I hadn't expected him to. I've seen dead people before and he looked like a classic case. Once, out of some sense of misplaced loyalty, I attended a friend's autopsy—well, most of it. There are some blurry spots, and the crystal-clear images I kept locked in a mental dungeon.

The man in the car looked to be in his mid-thirties, maybe a couple of years younger than my thirty-nine. He wore a white dress shirt that I doubted had ever been touched by an iron and blue jeans. His hair was sandy brown and curly. I didn't get close enough to see the color of his eyes. That was more information than I wanted.

I could see my reflection in the driver's side window. I saw the same shoulder length brown hair, narrow nose, and hazel eyes that were several degrees wider than they were in my bathroom mirror this morning—perhaps because there wasn't a corpse on the other side of the mirror.

The sound of rubber tires on asphalt caused me to turn. A patrol car with a uniformed officer stopped a few feet away. A moment later, a city issue Lincoln Continental—the chief's car—arrived. The Santa Rita police station sits less than fifty yards across the back parking lot that separates it from city hall. At best, it was a sixty-second drive. The uniformed officer stepped from his car and walked slowly in my direction. He took a moment to nod and offer a friendly, "Mayor," before returning his gaze to the macadam. It took me a second to realize that he was making sure he wasn't about to step on some piece of key evidence. I wondered what I had stepped in.

Satisfied that no shell casing or other evidence littered the lot, the officer walked to the Gremlin. Webb was two steps behind him as was another man I knew, Detective Judson West. When I saw Webb, my stomach soured.

"Madam Mayor," West said, with a wan smile. He stood a well proportioned six foot two, had hair black enough to shame coal and teeth that were whiter and straighter than piano keys. His dark eyes twinkled. At least I think I saw a twinkle. West is our lead robbery-homicide detective. He came to the city from the San Diego PD a little over six months ago. He's never talked about why he left the big city.

"Did you touch anything?" Chief Webb asked.

"I knocked on the window with my knuckle."

"That's it? You didn't try to open the car door?"

"It's locked. Besides, I know better than to put my fingerprints where they don't belong."

"How do you know the door is . . .?" I saw his gaze shift to the lock button on the door—it was down. Webb leaned over and peered through the side window to the door on the other side. I had done the same. He frowned.

West gave me a knowing smile. He knew of the tension between the chief and me and always seemed to find it entertaining. He turned to the officer. "All right, Bob, let's get the area taped off. In fact, I want the whole parking lot secured. No one in or out until we've searched the place and taken photos. You'd better call for some help. In the meantime, you'd better block the entrance with your car. The lot should start filling up any time now."

"Got it." Officer Bob reached for the microphone attached to the shoulder of his uniform and starting talking as he walked away.

"Not the way I planned to start the day," I said.

"You okay?" West asked.

"Fine. Just wasn't expecting a dead man in my parking spot."

I caught Webb looking our way and scowling. He was shorter than West, and his mane had grown comfortable with gray. He kept his hair combed back and held in place with some magical hair tonic. His eyes were an unhappy blue, and his face seemed frozen in disgust, as if he were on a castor oil diet. Red tinted his cheeks and the end of his nose.

Detective Judson West gave me one of his now famous smiles and inched his way over to his boss. I was still close enough to hear, but far enough away that I didn't have to see the dead man's face. I had seen enough of that.

"I don't suppose you've seen him before," Webb grumbled.

"No, and I'm pretty sure I'd remember."

"Not even during council meetings?"

The city council met every Tuesday evening at seven. It was a public meeting held in the chambers of city hall. Attendance was usually sparse with only a handful of citizens interested enough to pull themselves away from the television. Occasionally, a city measure would come up that would pack the place, but I could count those times on one hand. "Still no. I don't recall seeing the car either. I *know* I would remember that."

Even the chief nodded at that. He studied the car a little longer then turned to West. "It's all yours, Detective."

"Gee, thanks," West said. He smiled for a moment, then the grin disappeared. He was slipping into professional mode. I had seen it before. Half a year ago, I was embroiled in a mess of abductions and a murder. It ended badly, and I was still having nightmares. West had just started with our department, and I was his first case. I had seen what he could become when a mystery loomed before him.

Webb took a step back and watched West. The chief's chest seemed to swell as if watching his only son show up the neighbor's kid on the Little League field. West walked around the car, examining the paving, tires, door handles, windows, and everything else his eyes could fall upon. Then he stepped to the front of the car and placed his hand near the radiator grille. "Cold," he said. "It's been here for awhile." He tilted his head to the side. "Anyone else hear that?"

"Hear what?" I asked.

He paused before answering. "Music. I hear music."

I shook my head. I didn't hear anything. I stepped closer and picked up the hint of a tune. It was low, just loud enough to hear that something was there, but not enough to make out words. West walked to the passenger side of the car and looked in. "The keys are in the 'on' position. The music is coming from the radio." He straightened and turned at the sound of another police car arriving on the street. He waved the officer over. "Hey, Mitch, you got a Slim Jim in your patrol car, right? Bring it to me. Bring some gloves too."

A moment later, the officer was by West's side. He was holding a long flat piece of metal and a box of disposable latex gloves. West donned the gloves then took the flat tool. "Call the coroner, tell him we have some work for him, and then give Bob a hand with the crime-scene tape."

He studied the Gremlin again and then returned to the passenger side door. Without a word, he slipped the metal strip down between the window and rubber trim. He pushed, pulled, wiggled, and twisted the tool. "This is why I had to become a cop; I never could break into a car."

"It was a good choice," Webb said. "Benefits are better."

"Got it." He pulled up, and the door unlocked. He looked at me. "You want to guess why it is illegal for regular folk to own these?"

"I think I know."

"Yeah, but did you know there's an urban legend about police officers being killed while using them?" I admitted that I didn't. "The story goes that a car with side-collision air bags have shoved these devices into an officer's head. It's not true, of course. It makes a good story at a party."

"But you're still glad that a car this old doesn't have side airbags."

"I'll never admit it in public." He removed the tool and set it on the roof of the car. Using just one gloved finger, he pulled the handle and opened the door. I don't know what I was expecting, but I steeled myself for whatever came my way. The only difference I noticed was that I could now hear the music. The volume was weak.

"He must have had good ears," I said.

Webb looked at me and fought back a frown.

"I think the battery is dying," West said. He leaned in the car. I took a step back and shuddered. I couldn't see what he was doing. Seconds chugged by like hours and finally West came up for air. "I was wrong when I said the key was in the 'on' position; it's turned to 'accessories.'"

"Meaning?"

"Meaning that he pulled into your space, switched off the car, but left the key turned enough so the radio would still work."

"What else have you got?" Webb didn't say it, but even I knew what he was asking.

"Body indicates that death is recent, maybe six hours or so. The coroner will have to tell us that." West squinted at the corpse. "He certainly hasn't been sitting here over the weekend. The city hires private security for city buildings; don't they patrol the parking lots?" He looked to me for the answer.

"They're supposed to, but I don't oversee their work, the city manager does."

"I'd check into that."

"I plan to. Any clue as to why he died? I assume he died of natural causes—stroke, heart attack, something like that."

"Why would you assume that, Mayor?" Webb asked.

"The car was locked," I said. "It's a two-door hatchback. Only three ways in or out. It's like a locked room mystery."

"Ever lock your car without realizing it?" Webb asked.

I felt stupid. It wasn't hard to lock and close a door. If someone had murdered the poor man in the Gremlin, the murderer could easily have locked the door after exiting. I looked to West for help, but he only offered a raised eyebrow.

"Do you need me for anything else?" I asked. It was time to get out of Dodge before I said anything else stupid.

"Not now," West said, "but I'm sure I'll have questions. I just don't know what they are yet."

I pursed my lips and tried to act unflappable in front of the boys. "I need you to keep me apprised, Detective. Everyone in city hall is going to have questions. I need information if I'm going to sound intelligent." I caught Webb grinning. He was enjoying an unspoken joke.

BEYOND
TUESDAY
MORNING

A terrible tragedy.

One woman's discovery.

A chance to love again.

KAREN
BESTSELLING AUTHOR
OF *ONE TUESDAY MORNING*
KINGSBURY

ZONDERVAN

Karen Kingsbury

Karen Kingsbury is the author of over thirty titles, including *One Tuesday Morning*, and several other bestsellers, one of which was the basis for a CBS Movie-of-the-Week. With more than two million copies of her books in print, she is quickly becoming one of America's favorite inspirational authors. Kingsbury lives in Washington state with her husband, Don, and their six children, three of whom are adopted from Haiti.

A Word From the Author

True healing involves more than surviving a tragedy. It also requires that a person be able to move beyond that pain into the next season of life. Too often people experience hardship and then remain paralyzed, unable to move toward whatever God has next for them. *Beyond Tuesday Morning* takes Jamie Bryan from the point of survival to the place where she is able to live again.

In the Bible, God often details the two opposite sides of life. He calls those very different sides light and dark, or life and death. Deuteronomy tells us that we have before us the choice—life or death—and that we must choose life. *Beyond Tuesday Morning* is about taking stock of our situation and choosing life. It explores our willingness to trust Christ by moving into new life, even after walking through the darkest valley.

When I finished writing *One Tuesday Morning*, I was absolutely certain that Jamie Bryan's story wasn't complete. Time was needed for her to experience grief, to sort through what remained of the life she once knew. But once a few years had passed, it was time to revisit Jamie and the place she was in, and to write a story that would bring her from a very sad, painful place, to a new chapter in life, beyond that Tuesday morning.

I believe *Beyond Tuesday Morning* will engage readers and help them understand that it is possible to find new life, no matter what they've been through. Many will find that new life or the hope of it, even as they journey with Jamie Bryan through the pages of this, the next chapter in her story.

Karen Kingsbury

ONE

She was surviving; the commute proved that much.

Jamie Bryan took her position at the far end of the Staten Island Ferry, pressed her body against the railing, eyes on the place where the Twin Towers once stood. She could face it now, every day if she had to. The terrorist attacks had happened, the World Trade Center had collapsed, and the only man she'd ever loved had gone down with them.

Late fall was warmer than usual, and the breeze across the water washed over Jamie's face. If she could do this—if she could make this journey three times a week while seven-year-old Sierra was at school—then she could get through another long, dark night. She could face the empty place in the bed beside her, face the longing for the man who had been her best friend, the one she'd fallen for when she was only a girl.

If she could do this, she could do anything.

Jamie looked at her watch. Nine-fifteen, right on schedule.

Three times a week the routine was the same. From Staten Island across the harbor on the ferry, up through the park, past the brick walls that after September 11 were plastered with pictures of missing people, into the heart of lower Manhattan's financial district, past the cavernous crater where the Twin Towers had stood, to St. Paul's. The little church was a strangely out-of-place stone chapel with a century-old cemetery just thirty yards from the pit. A chapel that, for months after the attacks, had been a café, a hospital, a meeting place, a counseling office, a refuge, a haven to firefighters and police officers and rescue workers and volunteers, a place to pray and be prayed for. A place that pointed people to God.

All the things a church should be.

Never mind the plans for a new World Trade Center, or the city's designs for an official memorial. Never mind the tourists gathered at the ten-foot chain-link fence around the pit or the throngs gawking at the pictorial timeline pinned along the top of the fence— photos of the Twin Towers' inception and creation and place in history. Souvenir picture books might be sold around the perimeter of the pit, but only one place gave people a true taste of what had happened that awful day.

St. Paul's.

The ferry docked, and Jamie was one of the first off. When it was raining or snowing she took a cab, but today she walked. Streets in lower Manhattan teemed as they always had, but there was something different about the people. It didn't matter how many years passed, how many anniversaries of the attacks came and went.

The people of New York City would never be the same.

Yes, they were busy, still driven to climb the ladders or make a name for themselves in New York City. But for the most part they were more likely to make eye contact, and when they did, they were more likely to smile or nod or give some sort of sign that the bond was still there, that a city couldn't go through something like New Yorkers went through September 11 and not be changed forever.

Jamie breathed in hard through her nose and savored the sweet mix of seawater and city air. Jake would've liked this, the way she was facing the situation, allowing her pain to work for good in the lives of others. She had lived in paralyzing fear for so long, but now—now that she'd lost Jake—she could face anything. Not in her own strength, but because Jake's faith lived deep within her.

Funny how she'd come to be a volunteer at St. Paul's.

It was Captain Hisel's idea. He'd been Jake's boss, his mentor. He'd found Jake—or the man he *thought* was Jake—in the aftermath of the collapse of the towers. Of course the man hadn't been Jake at all but Eric Michaels, a Los Angeles businessman who came into Jamie's life by mistake. A man she believed was her husband for three agonizing months.

A man who'd gone home to his family three years ago without looking back. And rightfully so. Jamie had told only a few people the details of that tender, tragic time. Captain Hisel was one of them.

The captain became a special friend in the months and years since the terrorist attacks. At first they shared an occasional Sunday dinner, but since shortly after the first anniversary of the attacks they were together at least twice a week, volunteering at St. Paul's and sharing lunch or dinner. He was *Aaron* to her now, and the two of them had everything in common.

Or at least it seemed that way.

Jamie turned a corner and saw the old cemetery. It was clean now, free of the ash and debris that had gathered around the tombstones and remained there for months after the attacks. The island of Manhattan was a different place since that terrible Tuesday morning, more vulnerable, less cocksure. But warmer too. Stronger. For most of America, time might've dimmed the horror of what happened to New York City when the Twin Towers fell. But those who were there would always remember. The connection it gave Manhattan residents was undeniable.

A few feet in front of her, a street vendor nodded. "Nice day."

"Yes, it is." Jamie smiled and kept walking.

See. There it was again. Before September 11, a vendor wouldn't have made eye contact unless he wanted to push a hot dog or a bag of caramelized almonds. Now? Now the man was familiar. She saw him every time she volunteered at St. Paul's; he probably knew where she was headed, what she was doing.

Everyone in lower Manhattan knew about St. Paul's.

Jamie crossed the street, stopped, and turned—same as she did every day. Before she could enter St. Paul's Chapel, before she could open her heart to the picture-taking tourists and the quietly grieving regulars who couldn't stay away, she had to see for herself that the towers were really gone. It was part of the ritual. She had to look across the street at the grotesque gargantuan hole where the buildings once stood, had to remind herself why she was here and what she was doing, that terrorists really had flown airplanes into the World Trade Center and obliterated the buildings—and two thousand lives.

Because Jake had been one of those people, coming to St. Paul's kept him alive in some ways. Being at Ground Zero, helping out . . .

that was something Jake would've done. It was the very thing he'd been doing when he died.

Jamie let her gaze wander up into the empty sky, searching unseen floors and windows. Had he been on the way up—he and his best schoolboy buddy, Larry—trying to reach victims at the top? Or had he been partway down? She narrowed her eyes. If only God would give her a sign, so she would know exactly where to look.

She blinked and the invisible towers faded. Tears welled in her heart, and she closed her eyes. *Breathe, Jamie. You can do this. God, help me do this.*

A deep breath in through her nose. Exhale . . . slow and steady. *God . . . help me.*

My strength is sufficient for you, daughter.

She often prayed at this stage of the routine, and almost as often she felt God whispering to her, coaxing her, helping her along as a father might help his little girl. The way Jake had helped Sierra.

The quiet murmurs in the most hurting part of her soul were enough. Enough to give her strength and desire and determination to move ahead, to go through the doors of St. Paul's and do her part to keep the vigil for all she lost more than three years ago.

She turned her back to the pit and took determined steps beside the black wrought iron fence bordering the cemetery, around the corner to the small courtyard at the front of the chapel. The hallowed feeling always hit her here, on the cobbled steps of the little church. How many firefighters had entered here in the months after the attacks, firemen looking for food or comfort or a shoulder to cry on? How many had passed through it since the building had reopened, looking for hope or answers or a reason to grieve the tragedy even if it had never touched them personally?

Just inside the doors, Jamie turned to the left and stopped. There, scattered over a corner table, was a ragtag display of hundreds of items: yellowed photos, keepsakes, and letters written to victims of the attacks. She scanned the table, saving his picture for last. Beneath the photo of a balding man holding a newborn baby, the grin on his face ear to ear: *Joe, we're still waiting for you to come home* . . . Scribbled atop a wedding photo: *You were everything to me, Cecile; you still are* . . . Tacked to the side of a wallet-sized picture of a young FDNY guy:

Your ladder boys still take the field every now and then but it's not the same without you. Yesterday Saul hit a homer and every one of us looked up. Are you there?

Every time Jamie did this, her eyes found different letters, different snippets of pain and aching loss scattered across the display. But always she ended in the same place. At Jake's picture and the letter written by their daughter, Sierra.

Jake was so handsome, his eyes brilliant blue even in the poorly lit corner. *Jake . . . I'm here, Jake.* When there weren't too many people working their way into the building, she could stand there longer than usual. This was one of those days. Her eyes locked on her husband's, and for a moment he was there again, standing before her, smiling at her, holding his arms out to her.

Her fingers moved toward the picture, brushing the feathery photo paper as if it were Jake's face, his skin.

"Jake . . ."

For the briefest moment she was sure she could hear him. *Jamie, I'm not gone, I'm here. Come see for yourself.*

She drew her hand back and wrapped her arms around her waist. People had caught her touching his picture before; it made the volunteer coordinators nervous. As if maybe she wasn't ready to comfort others when she was still so far from healed herself.

She didn't mean to touch the photo; it just happened. Something about his eyes in the picture made him seem larger than life, the way he'd been before . . .

Before.

That was it, wasn't it? Life before September 11, and life after it. Two completely different lives. There were times when she thought she could hear Jake. His voice still rang in the corridors of her heart, the way it always would. Tears blurred her eyes and she gritted her teeth. She wouldn't break down here, not now. On his birthday or their anniversary, maybe. On the anniversary of September 11, of course. But if she was going to keep Jake's memory alive, she couldn't break down every time she volunteered.

She glanced at the letter, the one Sierra had written a few weeks ago on the third anniversary of the attack. Her daughter's other letters were safe in a scrapbook, a keepsake for Sierra so she wouldn't forget the closeness she'd shared with Jake. Every few months Sierra wrote a new note, and that one would replace the old one on the display table. The letter showed that Sierra still didn't know how her father had died. As far as she knew, her daddy didn't die on September 11 but three months later. In a fire, trying to save people trapped inside. It was a half-truth; the best Jamie could do under the circumstances.

She just hadn't known how to tell Sierra that the man who'd been living with them for three months wasn't really her father but a stranger. In the three years since Eric Michaels left them, Jamie had yet to figure out a way to talk about the subject. For that matter, Sierra still had a picture of herself standing next to Eric. Once, a little more than a year ago, Jamie had tried to take it down. She could still see the look on her daughter's face when she came running down the stairs into the kitchen, her eyes red with tears.

"My picture of me and Daddy is gone!"

Jamie felt awful about that one. She'd gone up with Sierra and pretended to look for it. That night while her daughter slept, Jamie took it from the closet where she'd hidden it and placed it on Sierra's dresser again. Right next to Jake's fire helmet.

Two other times she'd tried to replace it with other photos, pictures that actually were of Sierra and Jake.

"The one after Daddy got hurt is too sad," she'd tell Sierra. "Let's put it away, okay?"

But Sierra would move the other photos to her bookshelves, keeping the one of her and Eric on her dresser. "That's the last picture of me and Daddy. I want it there forever. Please, Mommy, don't make me move it."

The memory lifted.

Sierra had never even been to St. Paul's; she didn't know that's where her mother volunteered her time. The whole story about Eric and his time with them was getting harder to stand by. Deception wasn't Jamie's style, and lately she'd been feeling that one day soon she'd have to tell Sierra the truth. Her daughter deserved that much.

Jamie worked her gaze along her daughter's neat handwriting and read the letter for the hundredth time.

Dear Daddy, how are you doing up in heven? I'm doing good down here; I'm in second grade, and Mommy says I'm smartst in my class. But I'm not that smart cuz I have some things I don't know. Like how come you had to go to heven when I need you so much rite here? How come you had to help those peple in that fire? Why culdnt they wok out by themselfs. Somtimes I clos my eys and I remember how you lookd. Somtimes I remember budrfly kisses. But somtimes I forget. I love you. Sierra.

Sometimes she forgets.

That was the hardest part of all lately. The chapel entrance was empty, and Jamie closed her eyes. *God, don't let either of us forget Jake. He's with You, still alive somewhere in Paradise with You. But until we can all be together again, help Sierra remember him, God. Please. Help her—*

Someone tapped her shoulder, and she spun around, her breath in her throat. "Aaron!" She stepped back from the display table and forced a smile. "Hi."

"Hey." He backed up toward the wooden pews that filled the center of the chapel. "Someone wants to—"

Aaron looked past her at the picture of Jake, as if he'd only just realized the reason why she was standing there. For a long while he said nothing, then he looked at her, his eyes filled with a familiar depth. "I'm sorry. I didn't realize you were—"

"No, it's okay." She slipped her hands in the pockets of her sweater. "I was reading Sierra's letter. It's been three years; she's forgetting Jake."

Aaron bit his lip and let his gaze fall to the floor.

"It was bound to happen." She gave a slight shrug. The corners of her mouth lifted some, but the smile stopped there. "She was only four when he died."

"I know." A respectful quiet fell between them. "Still hard to believe he's gone."

"Yes." Once more she glanced at Jake's picture. "Still hard to believe."

She felt strangely awkward, the way she had back in high school when some boy other than Jake smiled at her or flirted with her. But

Aaron wasn't flirting with her, and she wasn't in high school . . . and Jake was dead.

But not really; not when he lived in her memory as fully as he'd once lived in her home.

No wonder the strange feeling, the hint of guilt at being caught looking at the picture of her husband. She'd felt this way before on occasion, though only when she was with Aaron. Even so, she refused to make too much of her emotions. They were bound to be all over the board, even if she and Aaron were only friends.

He nodded his head toward the center of the chapel. "There's a lady in the front pew; she could use your help. Husband was a cop, died in the collapse." His eyes met hers and held. Concern shone through, and the awkward feeling disappeared. "You ready?"

"Ready." Jamie fell in beside him and headed down one of the pews toward the other side of the chapel. She wanted to glance once more at Jake's picture, but she didn't.

He pointed to a blonde woman in the front row. "You got it?"

Jamie nodded. "What about you?"

"Over there." He glanced toward the back of the chapel. The memorial tables framed the perimeter of the room. A couple in their seventies stood near the back wall. "Tourists. Lots of questions."

They shared a knowing look—this was what they did at St. Paul's: being there for the people who came through the doors, whatever their reason—then they turned and went their separate ways.

With slow, hushed steps, Jamie came alongside the blonde woman. Many of the widows who visited St. Paul's had been there before, but this one wasn't familiar. Jamie sat down and waited until the woman looked at her.

"Hi, I'm Jamie Bryan; I'm a volunteer."

The woman's eyes were red and swollen, and though she opened her mouth, no words came. She lowered her head into her hands, and a few quiet sobs worked their way through her body.

Jamie put her hand on the woman's back. The woman was in her late forties, Jamie guessed, heavyset with an ocean of pain welling within her. When the woman's tears subsided, she sniffed and found Jamie's eyes. "Does . . . the pain ever go away?"

This was the hard part. Jamie was here at St. Paul's for one reason: to offer hope to those devastated by the losses of September 11. The problem was just what Martha White, the volunteer coordinator, had warned her from the beginning. She couldn't work through her own pain by giving advice to people about theirs.

"I'm fine," she'd told Martha. "I'm working through it, but I'm fine at St. Paul's."

Martha looked doubtful. "You tell me if it's too much." She wagged a motherly finger at Jamie. "You're a victim same as everyone else."

The coordinator's words came back to Jamie now, and she swallowed hard. What had the weeping woman just asked her? Did the pain ever go away?

Jamie looked from the woman to the front of the church, the place where the old ornate cross stood like an anchor. Without taking her eyes from it, Jamie gave a slow shake of her head. "No. The pain doesn't go away." She turned back to the woman. "But God helps us learn how to live with it."

Another wave of tears hit the woman. Her face contorted, and she pinched the bridge of her nose. "It still . . . feels like September 12. Sometimes I think it always will."

A strength rose from within Jamie. Every time she'd been needed in a situation like this one, God had delivered. Every time. She turned so she could see the woman better. "Tell me about your husband."

"He was a cop." She lifted one shoulder and ran the back of her hands beneath her eyes. "Everyone's always talking about the firemen, but the cops took a hit too."

Jamie had heard this before from the wives of other police officers. "Have you been around the chapel yet?"

"I just started when . . ." She held her breath, probably stifling another wave of sobs.

"It's okay to cry."

"Thank you." The woman's shoulders shook again. "This chapel . . . That's why I'm crying." She searched Jamie's eyes. "I didn't think anyone cared until I came here, and now . . ."

"Now you know the truth."

"Yes." The woman grabbed a quick breath and stared at a poster on a wall overhead. *Oklahoma Cares.* Beneath the banner title were hundreds of handprints from children who had experienced the bombing of the Murrow Building in Oklahoma City. One line read, *We love our police!* "I didn't come before because I didn't want to be angry at anyone. But this is where I need to be; I should've come a hundred times by now."

"I'm Jamie." She held out her hand, and the woman across from her took it. "What's your name?"

"Cindy Grammar." The woman allowed the hint of a smile. "Is it just me, or do you feel something here?"

"I feel it. Everyone who comes inside feels it."

"It's the only place where the memory of all those people still lives. You know, as a group."

"Exactly." Jamie folded her hands in her lap and looked around the chapel at the banners, then at the memorabilia lining the walls— items collected from the edge of the pit or left near the chapel steps. One day the city would have an official memorial to the victims of September 11. But for now, those two thousand people were remembered with grace and love at St. Paul's.

"This city loved my Bill. I could sense that the minute I walked in here."

"You're right." Jamie gave Cindy's hand a gentle squeeze. "And no one will forget what he did that day. He was a hero, Cindy. Same as the firefighters."

The conversation continued for nearly an hour before the woman felt ready to finish making her way around the inside of the building. By then her eyes were dry and she had shared the story of how she'd met her husband, how much they'd loved each other. Jamie knew the names of the woman's two sons, and the fact that they both played high school football.

"Thanks, Jamie." The woman's expression was still filled with sorrow, but now it was also tinged with gratitude and peace. "I haven't felt this good in months."

Jamie's heart soared. Her job was to bring hope to the hopeless, and to do it in Jake's name. Again and again and again. She took Cindy's hands again. "Let's pray, okay?"

The woman squirmed. "I'm . . . I'm not sure about God, Jamie."

"That's okay." Jamie's smile came from her heart, from the place that understood God the way Jake had always wanted her to understand. "God's sure about you."

"Really?" Doubt colored Cindy's eyes.

"Really. We don't have to pray; just let me know." Jamie bit her lip, waiting.

"I want to." The woman knit her brow together. "I don't know what to say."

Jamie gave the woman's hand a gentle squeeze. "I'll say it." She bowed her head and began, the way she had dozens of times over the past two years. "God, we come to You because You know all things. You are sovereign and mighty and You care about us deeply. Help Cindy believe in You, Lord. Help her to understand that You hold a flashlight as we walk through the valley of the shadow of death. And let her find new life in You. In Jesus' name, amen."

Jamie opened her eyes.

A fresh sort of peace filled Cindy's face. She leaned closer and hugged Jamie. "I'll be back."

Jamie smiled. "I know."

The woman stood and headed for the outer rim of the chapel with a promise to return some day so that maybe the two could talk—and even pray again.

When she was finally alone, Jamie's hands trembled. Her legs were stiff from sitting for so long. Meetings like that were emotionally draining, and Jamie wanted water before she talked to anyone else.

But before she could reach the stairs, another woman approached her, four young teenage girls in tow, each holding a notebook. "Hi, maybe you could help us."

"Of course." Jamie gave the group her full attention. "What would you like to know?"

"We're a homeschool group and—" she looked at the girls— "each of the students has a list of questions for you. They want to know how St. Paul's was instrumental in serving the people who cleaned up the pile of debris after the towers collapsed."

"Okay." Jamie smiled, but something grated against her heart. The pile of debris? Jake had been in that pile. It was okay for *her* to call it that, but these people were . . . they were on a quest for details, like so many reporters. She ignored her irritation and directed the group to the nearest pew. "Let's sit here and we can talk."

School groups were common, and always needed help from volunteers. They wanted to know how many hundreds of gallons of water were given out—more than four thousand; how many different types of services were offered free to the work crew—podiatry, massage therapy, counseling, chiropractic care, nursing care, and optometry among others; and what sort of impact did St. Paul's and its volunteers have on the work crew—a dramatic one.

The questions continued, but they weren't out of line. By the time Jamie was finished talking with the group, she regretted her first impression. The girls were well-mannered, the parent sensitive to the information Jamie shared. It was nearly noon when the group went on their way. Jamie scanned the pews first, and then the perimeter of the chapel. She was thirsty, but the visitors came first. The week she trained as a volunteer Martha had made that clear.

"Look for fires to put out." A tiny woman with a big mouth and a heart as vast as the Grand Canyon, Martha was particularly serious about this detail. "Look for the people breaking down and weeping, the ones sitting by themselves in a pew. Those are the ones you should approach. Just so they know you're there."

No fires at the moment.

Aaron was across the room, talking to another pair of tourists. At least his conversations looked less intense than the one she'd had with Cindy. She trudged up the stairs to the volunteers' break room. An open case of water bottles sat on the table; she took one and twisted off the lid. Chairs lined the area, but she was tired of sitting. She leaned against the stone wall and looked up at the aged stained glass.

Funny, the way Martha had said it. *Fires to put out.* It was one more way Jamie was keeping Jake's memory alive. No, she didn't deal with flames and fire hoses. But she was putting out fires all the same. He would've been proud of her.

In fact, if he'd survived, he'd be right here at St. Paul's with her. All the more reason to volunteer as long as the chapel was open. It gave her purpose, and in that sense it wasn't only a way to keep Jake's memory, his sacrifice, alive.

It was a way to keep herself alive too.

BREAKER'S REEF

BOOK FOUR

Terri Blackstock

ZONDERVAN

Bestselling Author of CAPE REFUGE

Terri Blackstock

Terri Blackstock (www.terriblackstock.com) is the bestselling author of the Newpointe 911 and Sun Coast Chronicles suspense series and other books, including *Cape Refuge, Emerald Windows, Seaside,* and her novels with Beverly LaHaye.

A Word From the Author

Dear Friend,

Have you ever been overcome with regrets in your life, reaping the harvest of the sins you have sown, and wondering if God's promises to forgive and cleanse really apply to you? In Breaker's Reef, ex-con Sheila Caruso experiences those same thoughts when her sins 'effects trickle down to her children. As she struggles with her past failures and the terrible choices that brought her to where she is today, she discovers that one more choice-the right one-can change the course of her life. As she desperately tries to right the wrongs of her past, she finds that Christ is with her, helping her navigate her way through her mess, setting her chaos in order, and changing her very nature.

In *Breaker's Reef,* I wanted to show that a person steeped in sins-past and present-can't truly repent until they hate those sins with even more passion than they once loved them. Then, and only then, can Christ show us His true redemption. As I wrote this book, the Lord showed me new things about my own redemption and the righteousness I can have in Him. My hope is that He will show the same things to you.

Terri Blackstock
www.terriblackstock.com

CHAPTER

1

Chief Matthew Cade rarely considered another line of work, but the 4:30 a.m. phone call about the dead teenage girl made him long for a job as an accountant or electrician—some benign vocation that didn't require him to look into the eyes of grieving parents. He sat on the side of his bed, rubbing his eyes as he clutched the phone to his ear.

"She's from Cape Refuge, Chief." Myrtle, his night shift dispatcher, sounded shaken. "That new guy, Scott Crown, just found her floating in a boat on the Tybee side of the river. Looks like a homicide."

Cade braced himself. "Who is it, Myrtle?"

"Didn't give me a name yet. If they know it, they're keeping it off the radio for now. But Chief Grant from Tybee is hot about how Crown handled things, and he wanted you to come to the scene as soon as you can."

"All right, give me the address." Oswald, Cade's cat, jumped onto his lap, purring for attention as Cade fumbled for a pen and jotted the address down. The cat stepped onto the bed table and plopped down on the notepad. "So what is it Crown did?"

"I'm not clear on that, Chief. But he's young. Go easy on him."

He clicked the phone off and thought about the nineteen-year-old rookie. Crown joined the force straight out of the academy; he hadn't even been in Cade's department a week. His zeal to be the best cop in the department had led to a few mishaps already, but nothing serious. Cade knew he just needed to give the kid some time to grow into his position. But what had he done to aggravate the neighboring chief?

He got up, wincing at the arthritic ache he always felt in his leg first thing in the morning. It had healed from the multiple fractures he'd sustained in an injury a year ago—and he'd overcome his limp for the most part—but the mornings always reminded him how far he'd come.

He got dressed and hurried out to his truck. It was cool for May, but he knew it would warm up to the upper eighties by the end of the day. Life would go on as it always did—murder or not. As he drove across the bridge that connected Cape Refuge to Tybee Island, his mind raced with the faces of teenage girls who'd grown up here. Whoever this girl was, the murder would have a rippling effect, shattering her family and shaking her friends. There would be a life-size hole in the heart of the small town.

He found the site and pulled up to the squad cars parked there. One of the Tybee officers met him as he got out. "Oh, it's you, Chief Cade. I didn't recognize you in your truck."

"Where's Chief Grant?" he asked.

The man pointed to the riverbank, and Cade saw him with the medical examiner looking over the body.

As he approached, Cade saw the girl lying on the grass. She was small, maybe a hundred pounds, and looked as if someone had laid her down there, her arms out from her body, her knees together and bent to the side. In the flickering blue light, he couldn't yet see her face, and her hair was wet, long ... He walked closer, and Keith Parker, the medical examiner, looked up at him. "Hey, Cade. You recognize her?"

Chief Grant handed him a flashlight, and Cade stooped down and illuminated her face. His heart plunged. She was Alan Lawrence's girl, Emily. She couldn't be more than fifteen. Cade didn't think she'd even gotten her license yet.

Anger stung his eyes, and he rubbed his jaw. His throat was tight as he swallowed. Who could have done this? Who would have wanted to end the life of an innocent, sweet girl whose parents loved her?

He cleared his throat. "Yeah, her name's Emily Lawrence. Her parents are Alan and Marie." He paused, trying to steady his voice. "You know the cause of death?"

"Gunshot," Grant said. "Looks like she was shot in another location, then apparently brought here and put into that boat. Your man found her."

Cade stood and looked in the direction Grant nodded. Scott Crown stood with the other cops, answering questions. His uniform was wet, and he looked shaken and nervous. Cade felt sorry for the kid. Odds were he hadn't expected to find a dead girl his first week on the job.

"Unfortunately," the Tybee chief went on, "your man compromised the evidence. Moved the body out of the boat before he called us. Got her wet trying to get her onto the shore. Who knows what evidence might have been washed off? I would think you'd train your people better than that."

Cade's anger shifted from the faceless killer to the rookie. "What was he even doing over here? He was supposed to be patrolling Cape Refuge."

"He saw the boat floating in the river between the two islands, saw that someone was in it. Right then he should have called my department instead of coming onto my turf and handling the matter himself."

Cade sighed and looked toward the kid again. He'd had reservations about hiring someone so young right out of the academy, but Crown was Joe McCormick's nephew. When his detective vouched for the kid, Cade decided to give him the benefit of the doubt. But he'd recognized Crown's hero complex his first day on the job. He was something of a loose cannon, and Cade had wondered if he could trust him to follow the rules.

Apparently, he couldn't.

He crossed the grass toward Crown. The kid turned, saw him, and burst into his explanation. "Chief, I know I did wrong. It was stupid. I don't even know what I was thinking. But there were vultures, and I thought there must be a dead animal in the boat . . . I crossed the bridge and came over here—"

"Your first mistake," Cade said.

"But if I hadn't, they might not have found her!"

"Crown, if you had called Tybee to tell them what you saw, they would have been there in minutes. Not only did you step outside of our jurisdiction, but you botched up the evidence."

The kid looked at the cops around him, as if humiliated that he'd been reamed in front of them. "I didn't botch it up."

"Yes, you did! I *know* they taught you in the academy never to move a body. And then you go and wash off the evidence!"

In the light of the police cars' headlights, he could see the kid's face turning red. "Okay, I'm sorry! I got out to the boat and recognized the girl. I wasn't sure she was dead. I was trying to *save* her!"

"You should have checked before you got her out of the boat!"

"Right." Crown's voice rose as he shot back. "So let me get this straight. Next time I see a girl dying in a boat, I'm supposed to sit on my hands until the right people get there? I thought we were emergency personnel. I thought it was our job to *save* lives!"

Crown was livid, stepping over his bounds. Clearly, Cade wasn't going to teach him anything right here in front of his peers. Besides, there was a dead girl lying there—and a killer to be identified. He didn't have time to deal with the rookie.

"Go back to the station, Crown. Wait for me there."

"I don't *want* to go back. *I* found her!"

Cade stepped nose-to-nose with the kid, speaking through his teeth. "Now, Crown. If I hear one more word, you're fired."

Crown backed down then and, without another word, stormed off to his car. Cade watched him until he drove away, then breathed a frustrated sigh and turned back to the body.

Emily. He remembered watching her at the Hanover House Easter egg hunt when she was three. She'd practically tripped over the "hidden" eggs and celebrated when she found her first one, while those around her snatched up all the rest. Who would want her dead?

He went back to his car and radioed in. "Chief Cade here. Get all available units to secure the bank of the Bull River across from where the body was found. I don't want anyone traipsing through there until I have a chance to get over there. We don't know which side the boat was put in on."

The radio crackled, and Myrtle's voice rasped across the airwaves. "Will do, Chief." As she began radioing the other cars on duty, he went back to the body and stooped down next to the medical examiner. "Where's the gunshot wound, Keith?"

The ME pointed to the hole in her stomach. "No exit wound, so it probably didn't happen at close range. The bullet's still in there. But she was shot hours ago. Bled out before she was put into the boat."

Cade stood, a sick feeling twisting in his gut as he anticipated having to go to her home and break the news to her parents. They might not even know she was missing yet. If they'd gone to bed before her curfew, they wouldn't know until morning. But if they were more diligent, as he knew Alan was, they might be up even now, waiting to confront her when she came in.

In a million years, they would never expect news like this.

He wished he was in charge of the investigation, but the murder hadn't happened on his turf. Still, he looked over the body as the medical examiner knelt beside her.

"That a bruise on her jaw?" Cade asked.

"Yep. Several more on her arms and legs. There was definitely a struggle. And look at this." He pointed to the chafed skin around her mouth. "Looks like duct tape was pulled off of her mouth and wrists."

It had clearly been an abduction. Cade looked across the dark water. Was there a murderer still lurking on his island, looking for young girls?

"We need to notify the family, Cade."

He turned to Grant. "I'll do it. They're friends of mine."

"I'm waiting for the GBI to get here. I'll need their help on this."

Cade knew the GBI, Georgia's Bureau of Investigation, had the resources to solve this case. He was glad they'd been notified so early.

"One of our detectives is going to need to go through her room, see what we can find," Grant said. "If you can just break the news to the parents, then my detective or the state's men can take it from there."

Right. Let me do the dirty work, then be on my way. "That's fine. I'll seal off her room, make sure nobody goes in there."

He strode back to his truck, trying to get his head together. How was he going to break it to them? The muscles in the back of his neck were rock hard, and his jaw hurt as he ground his teeth together. What would he say? How would he phrase it?

Lord, give me the words.

As he drove his pickup back to Cape Refuge, Cade rehearsed the hated speech in his mind. *Alan and Marie, I'm afraid I have some bad news . . .*

GILBERT MORRIS

Award-Winning Author of EDGE OF HONOR

CHARADE

HIS PLAN FOR REVENGE
WAS PERFECT . . . ALMOST

ZONDERVAN

Gilbert Morris

Gilbert Morris is one of today's best-known Christian novelists, specializing in historical fiction. His bestselling works include *Edge of Honor* (winner of a Christy Award in 2001), *Jacob's Way*, the House of Winslow series, the Appomattox series, and The Wakefield Saga. He lives in Gulf Shores, Alabama, with his wife, Johnnie.

A Word From the Author

It's not clear which is more dangerous—not getting what we want, or getting what we long for. So often we long for things that are not in God's plan for our lives, and if we do get them, they never satisfy. In my novel *Charade*, Ollie Davis longs for a change in his physical appearance, for fame, and for riches. When by what seems to be a miracle, he achieves all these goals, he is shocked to discover that they do not bring him happiness.

In this novel, I wanted to dramatize the warning given by a wise man, "Be careful what you pray for—you may get it!"

Ollie Davis lives in our time and our place. Like many in our culture, he is tantalized by the media which promises him that satisfaction and happiness lie in possessions. But Ollie discovers that real joy does not reside in bank accounts, fast cars, and other symbols of wealth.

I wrote this novel to highlight the wisdom that comes from God's Word, "Seek ye first the Kingdom of God, and all these things shall be added unto you."

Gilbert Morris

Chapter 1

I, Ollie William Benson, am obsessed by mirrors. It's not that I want to collect them, or that I'm fascinated by them. *Au contraire!* I wish that I lived in a world where there were *no* mirrors. The problem, you see, is that when I look into a mirror, I see myself.

That may sound strange to "normal" people. Obviously, mirrors were made for just such a purpose. But ever since I became aware that I was different from other people, I've hated mirrors and avoided them whenever possible. When I say "different from other people," you probably think I have a hideous deformity—maybe something like John Merrick, the Elephant Man—but I don't. On the other hand, maybe I really do, for at the height of exactly six feet I weigh four hundred and six pounds.

I don't think anyone of normal size understands what it means to be obese. You have to be there. When a normal person flies in an airplane, he buys one ticket. But I have to go first class or buy *two* tickets. I can't waltz into Tommy Hilfiger's and buy a shirt or a pair of slacks. I have to find a shop on a back street that makes clothing that could be worn by whales with arms and legs.

I guess you have to be obese in order to recognize the disgust and pity that flickers in the eyes of people when you meet them for the first time. I'm sure that some doctors can feel compassion for the obese, but most of them I've met seem to have a covert attitude of: *The big tub of lard, he ate himself into this. It's his own fault.* They smile and say comforting things, but that's what they really think: *He brought it on himself.*

So that's my problem. I'm fat, shake like a bowl of jelly, and at the age of twenty-nine, when most young guys are at their best, I spend my life hiding from the world in my little cubicle at the rear of Maxie's Electronics. Then I scurry home to my apartment and pull up the drawbridge to keep people out. I cook meals that I know I shouldn't eat but eat anyway, wondering from time to time what it would be like to be a normal person. What would it be like to have a girlfriend? What would it be like to put on a pair of swimming trunks and not feel like a pale hippopotamus?

So that's why I hate mirrors, and that's why I don't have any in my apartment—except in the bathroom. I got rid of all the rest, but that one was built in as part of the decor. It's three feet wide and goes all the way to the ceiling. It must have been designed by a body builder or a beauty queen, someone who loved to look at themselves.

As soon as I moved in, I knew I couldn't face taking a shower, stepping out, and seeing a mountain of gluttonous fat, which is what I've become. My solution was simple enough. I simply bought a life-size poster of John Wayne, a still taken from *Stagecoach*, his first big hit. You've seen it—the one where he's carrying the rifle and standing beside his saddle. I fastened it over the mirror with Scotch tape so that when I got out of the tub, instead of seeing myself, I saw the Duke.

Over the next couple of years, I changed the poster several times. Steve McQueen did his duty for a few months, and he was succeeded by Randolph Scott—an actor nobody remembers except us old-movie buffs. Lee Van Cleef was one of my favorites, and he lasted nearly six months. The most recent one was Clint Eastwood wearing his Mexican serape and his flat-crowned hat, with a thin cigar clenched between his teeth. I suppose a shrink would probably have something to say about how all of these dudes were what I was not—strong, virile, lean, mean, and ready to face anybody down before or after breakfast. Well, let them say it.

When I think about all that happened, it seems to have started that Friday night with the mirror in the bathroom. Just an ordinary day, nothing special. I got home early, took off my sweaty clothes, for it's hot in Memphis in July, and threw them in the hamper. I turned the water on as hot as I could stand it, and soon the room was filled with steam. It was almost as good as being in a sauna—or so I thought, although I'd never been in one. That's another of those things I would never expose myself to—getting into a small room naked with normal men.

By the time I was about ready to vaporize, I turned the water off, flung the curtain back, and stepped out of the shower. Then I stopped dead still.

Clint Eastwood wasn't there—

I was there!

The steam had peeled the Scotch tape from the mirror and the poster lay coiled in an obscene sprawl on the floor. I stared at myself, unable to move. No way could I avoid seeing the double and triple chins, the flab that hung on me, and the stomach that looked as if it had been inflated by a huge bicycle pump. Everything about me was disgusting, and suddenly I was trembling uncontrollably. I grabbed a towel and wheeled away from the mirror, trying to forget—but I have a very good memory, *too* good in fact. Even as I toweled myself down, a scene flashed on the back of my eyes in full color and with stereophonic sound. I could even smell the odors of the weight room where I had gone to try once again to lose weight. I was on the stair-climber, which I had set at the very lowest level. The little red dots were all across the bottom of the screen, and I was huffing and puffing, trying not to fall off.

Then a girl eighteen or nineteen, wearing a tight, white Spandex top and black shorts that clung to her like an extra skin, stepped onto the machine next to mine. She set it on max, with all the red dots at the top, and as soon as it was going full speed, she moved with an easy rhythm.

I remembered that when she finally stopped the machine, she turned and looked at me, fat and huge and gross and sweating like crazy. She smiled, showing a lot of teeth, and said cheerfully, "Keep at it. You'll make it."

But I saw the pity and disgust in her eyes, and when she walked over to her friend on another stair-climber, I heard her whisper, "Hippo will never make it, he's too far gone."

I shoved that memory back into a dark closet (knowing full well it wouldn't stay there). Well, we all have things to get over. I dried and put on my underwear, and then I went back to the bathroom. The rodeo guys say when you get thrown by a horse, you go get right back on.

I picked Clint up, fastened him back using twice as much tape as I'd used before, then walked over to the lavatory and studied my face in the small mirror that hung there for shaving. What did I look like under all that excess flesh? The Shadow knows, I guess, but nobody else. I had grown so used to seeing my fat face that it was just a blob to me. I took in the light brown hair and the blue eyes and the beard that was a mistake. Rather fair skin. Just a skull covered with doughy fat.

And on that night, I had a date—which didn't happen often. Just the thought of going out with a woman scared me silly. My hands were not steady when I trimmed the beard, but I combed my hair, went into my bedroom, and began to dress.

I'd bought new clothes for this date—from the Big Men's Shop, of course. They were the most expensive threads I'd ever bought, a pair of charcoal slacks and a navy-blue sport jacket, single vested, more or less a blazer. I sat down and put on the new Johnson-and-Murphy shoes, a hundred bucks a shoe, then I braced myself and walked back into the bathroom and stared at myself in the mirror. For a moment I didn't move, then I said out loud, "Ollie Benson, you look like a fat, ugly baby with a stupid beard!"

The sound of the phone ringing turned me around, and I walked out of the bathroom and picked it up. "Hello?"

"Hey, Ollie, are you about ready?"

"Jimmy . . . I . . . don't think I can make it."

"Can't make it? Hey, what are you talking about, man, you *gotta* make it!"

"Look, Jimmy, I just don't date. You know that. I don't know why I ever let you talk me into this."

Jimmy Douglas was my best friend. He worked the counter and dealt with customers at Maxie's while I did all the work on the computers in the back. He was as small and lean as I was gobby fat, a swift talker whereas I was pretty silent, a sharp dresser where I wore whatever I could get on. Pretty much the opposite of everything I am. Still, we'd worked together for three years, and he was the closest thing I had to a friend. He had been after me for some time to go out on a date with him, and finally, in a weak moment, I had agreed.

"Look." Jimmy had a sharp, staccato voice and a habit of repeating himself. "Look, you gotta go. I mean you *gotta* go, man! You can't stay in that stupid room all your life. Get with it—*get with it*, man! I ain't takin' no for an answer. We got these girls lined up, and you know how hard I been tryin' to get Tammy to go out with me."

"I know, Jimmy." All I had heard for the past three months was the name Tammy McNeil. She had been the second runner-up in the Miss Tennessee contest the previous year, and Jimmy had been in ecstasy when she had said she'd go out with him. "The catch is," he said, "she's got this cousin from Ohio or Nebraska or somewhere—some dumb state that ends with a vowel." Just like Jimmy to not know the difference between Ohio and Nebraska. "She won't go out with me unless I find a date for her friend."

"Jimmy—"

"Don't say it—don't say it, Ollie. Look, you gotta do it. We're friends—we're friends, ain't we?"

"Sure we are, but I'm just no good with girls."

"Ah, you'll be great with this one, you'll be great. Tammy says she's smart—like you. She's gettin' her degree in sociology—or maybe it was psychology or something else. Anyway, she's real smart, and you two will get on fine. Come on now, don't let me down."

A sense of doom settled on me. I had no happy memories of going out with girls. I had tried a blind date three times, and those three times were reminiscent of the sinking of the *Titanic*, the fall of the Alamo, and the destruction of Hiroshima. Each of those three times, I had vowed never to go out again on a blind date—but now I heard myself saying fatalistically, "All right, Jimmy, but I can tell you it won't work."

"Sure it'll work—sure it'll work! We'll make it fine. Come on now. We don't want to be late."

I hung up the phone and walked slowly around my apartment. It wasn't much, to tell the truth. The living room had a couch, a chair, a huge TV, a window, and a door.

The bedroom was pretty much the same: four walls, a floor, and a ceiling, along with a bed and a chest of drawers and a small closet.

Of the two rooms where I actually lived, the computer room was my hiding place. In there, I was king of the world. I stepped inside it now, glanced around, and wished fervently that I could simply go in, sit down, and play with the computers.

My latest toy was the newest, fastest Powerbook made, and I ran it lean and mean for maximum speed. It was less than an inch thick and weighed less than five pounds. With my discount, I got it for only two thousand dollars with all the bells and whistles. Maybe I loved it because it was so small and I was so huge. And what would Freud make of that little gem?

The other room I spent my *real* life in was the kitchen. It was spotless and contained every expensive laborsaving gadget devised by the mind of man for the art of cooking. After computers, cooking took up most of the rest of my life, and once again I felt myself longing simply to create a magnificent meal and sit down and eat until I was groggy.

But Jimmy was my friend, and I had promised. So I left the apartment and waited until Jimmy pulled up in his '01 Infinity. I opened the door and got in and, as always, felt the car tilt to starboard. Jimmy grinned and reached over and punched me on the arm. "Hey, now," he yelped. "We're gonna get with it tonight. Watch our smoke!"

"Yep, we're gonna get with it," I tried to say cheerfully. And then I thought, *Maybe it'll be different this time. The girl may be homely, but maybe she likes to talk. Maybe we'll hit it off.* I nourished that little fantasy as Jimmy sped around the streets of Memphis, until finally he pulled up in front of a tan brick apartment building on Sycamore Street.

"This is it," Jimmy said. "Come on, let's go get those women!"

I got out of the car and followed Jimmy, who was practically dancing with excitement. We mounted the steps, Jimmy rang the bell, and almost at once the door opened.

"Hey, Tammy, this is my friend I told you about, Ollie Benson. Ollie, this is Tammy McNeil, the almost Miss Tennessee."

"I'm glad to know you."

"Pleased to meet you," I muttered, but I had seen the look in her eyes and the quick contraction of her mouth at the corners. How well I knew that look! Translated, it meant, *You brought this fat slob as a date for my friend? You must be crazy!*

Jimmy noticed nothing; he was too busy telling Tammy how gorgeous she was. Then another young woman stepped out and I heard Tammy say, "This is Lorraine Patterson. Lorraine, this is—what'd you say your name is?"

"Ollie Benson. I'm glad to know you, Lorraine."

"Glad to know you too, Ollie."

Lorraine was an even worse actress and less adept at covering her feelings than Miss-Almost-Tennessee. The disgust that flared in her eyes shut all my systems down. Even Jimmy must have seen it! Her jaw muscles tightened as she ground her teeth together, and I would have given the most expensive computer I had to be away from this place.

"Well, come on," Jimmy said. "Time's a-wastin'—time's a-wastin'!"

I walked woodenly toward the car, opened the door for Lorraine, then walked around and got in the other side. This time the car tilted to port, and the springs squealed under my weight. Jimmy got in, started the car up, and said, "Hold onto your hats, kids, we're gonna get loose tonight!" Jimmy has a real way with words.

Jimmy rattled on to Tammy, and soon I felt I had to make some attempt at conversation. "I understand you're in college."

"Yes, I'm a psych major."

"That must be very interesting."

"What do you do?" The woman looked at me. She was a little over-weight herself—nothing like me, of course. She had brown hair, rather smallish brown eyes, and was pretty in a sort of bovine way. Her eyes were what frightened me. She looked at me as if I were a mouse in a cage being prepared for some sort of experiment. She said suddenly, "Have you ever tried to get professional help for your problem?"

I could not speak. Nobody had ever said anything like that. I'm sure they thought it, and they no doubt talked about it when I wasn't there, but Lorraine Patterson came right out with it.

"Not really," I mumbled.

"You should. There are some marvelous new treatments—psycho-logical, of course. You realize, don't you, that obesity isn't a physical prob-lem? You have a severe *psychological* problem. All you need to do is get that solved, and you'll be perfectly normal."

For the rest of the ride to the club, she talked about how many fat people had been helped by psychology. I couldn't think of a word to say and was relieved when we finally got to the nightclub.

Lorraine didn't wait for me to come open her door. Jimmy grabbed Tammy's arm and the two fled, then Lorraine followed and I had to hurry to catch up.

By the time we got inside I was sick. I knew I'd made a bad mistake but couldn't think of any way out of it. It was rather a small place, but it made up for its lack of size by a great deal of noise. A band of some sort was making something that sounded vaguely like music. To me it was almost torture. I followed the other three to a table where we sat down, and a waiter hovered over us, saying, "What's it gonna be?"

Jimmy ordered a cocktail, Tammy a martini, and Lorraine a mar-garita. The waiter looked at me, and I said, "Just a Coke, please."

The waiter stared at me. "Just a Coke? That's all?"

"That's all."

In disgust he left, and Jimmy said quickly, "Ollie here doesn't drink."

"How nice for him," Lorraine snapped.

The drinks came, and we all tasted them, and then at once Jimmy was up saying, "Let's dance, Tammy."

He hauled her onto the dance floor, and Lorraine got up. "Well, I guess we may as well dance too."

"I—I don't dance."

She stared at me in disbelief, and I could see that she'd had enough of Ollie Benson to last her the rest of her life. She sat again, picked up her drink, and began working on it.

Einstein said something about time being relative, and the next hour proved his theory true. Time crept by, each second lasting half an hour. Jimmy and Miss Tennessee danced, and I tried valiantly to carry on some sort of a conversation, but Lorraine grew more silent and as frigid as polar ice as time went on.

Finally I excused myself and went to the men's room. I stayed there as long as I decently could, but there's a limit to what you can pretend to do in a men's room. When I got back to the table I saw a tall guy standing there, smiling down at the others. When Tammy looked up and saw me, she said, "Oh, yes, this is—what's your name again?"

"Ollie Benson."

"Oh, yeah. Ollie, this is Carl Johnson. He works for a movie studio in Hollywood."

We shook hands and Jimmy said, "Yeah, they're shooting a film here right down on Beale Street. Hey, Carl, sit down and join us."

"No, I'd be the odd man out."

Johnson was a well-built man with slightly curly hair and a cleft chin. He turned to move, but I said quickly, "Hey, why don't you stay, Carl?" To the others, I said, "I'm not feelin' well. If you don't mind, I think I'll go home."

"That's too bad," Lorraine said quickly, "but you should take care of yourself."

"Yeah," Tammy said just as quickly, "good to meet you."

Jimmy looked worried. "You okay? I'll take you home."

"No, I'll catch a cab. You guys have a good time."

They all made "sorry-about-that" noises as I turned and left. When I stepped outside, I felt like the Count of Monte Cristo when he finally broke out of his prison. Quick as I could, I got a taxi and left the scene of the crime.

When I got home I shucked off all my clothes, threw them on the floor, and put on my usual costume in the summer—a pair of shorts, a Hawaiian sport shirt with enough material to make the sails for the *Mayflower*, and soft chenille flip-flops.

I went into the kitchen, got a king-sized bag of Doritos, a box of Little Debbies, and a quart of chocolate milk. Then I went to the computer room and sat down in my chair. It was a massive office chair, the biggest one I could find—the only one I'd ever seen big enough to carry my weight.

I ate a half-dozen Little Debbies, washing them down with chocolate milk, then I reached out and touched the mouse.

When I begin to work with a computer, something comes over me. I'm in another world, almost like a parallel universe. It's like that movie *The Wizard of Oz*. At first everything is gray and unhappy, and then suddenly Dorothy wakes up in a Technicolor world. I'm lost in the beauty of the computer and would love to stay there for all eternity.

I don't know how long I had worked, probably two or three hours. Once again, Mr. Einstein's relativity kicked in. I looked up just in time to see my mouse, the real one with fur. She had started visiting me maybe two months earlier, but by this time she came every night. She had lost all fear of me. In the darkness of the room, illuminated only by the screen of the computer, her eyes were as silver as the screen itself. I reached down and gave her a morsel of a Little Debbie and watched as she sat up and delicately nibbled at it. Her paws were tiny and a miracle if I ever saw one. I remembered that Walt Whitman once said, "A mouse is miracle enough to stagger sextillions of infidels." How right you were, Walter!

Suddenly the memory of the evening came back, and a great wave of bitterness swept over me, a tsunami of rage and frustration. I thought of Scarlett lifting her hands to heaven and vowing, "I'll never go hungry again!"

So that night, when it all started, I closed my eyes for a time. Then I opened them and looked at the mouse, and I said, "Miss Mousie, I'll never let a woman humiliate me again!"

Miss Mousie stared at me for an instant and then calmly resumed nibbling at the Little Debbie.

BRANDILYN COLLINS

Bestselling Author of BRINK OF DEATH

Dead of Night

ZONDERVAN

HIDDEN FACES SERIES

Brandilyn Collins

Brandilyn Collins is the bestselling author of *Brink of Death, Eyes of Elisha,* and other novels. She and her family divide their time between the California Bay Area and Coeur d'Alene, Idaho. Visit her website at www.brandilyncollins.com.

A Word From the Author

Too many times, we Christians find ourselves mired in defeat. We either think our problems are too big for God to handle, or we simply don't think to give them to God at all. In *Dead of Night*, the third book in my Hidden Faces suspense series, Annie Kingston and other Christians in her city are faced with the terrifying evil of a serial killer. Where is God in the midst of this crisis? What can Christians do to help?

Dead of Night is an intense story that dares to pry open the mind of evil. Even more so, it's the story of God's power—unleashed through prayer—over that evil. We live in a fallen, dark world. But we Christians must not forget that our Lord is ultimately in control, even in the blackest moments. I wanted to write a story that grips readers enough, shakes them up enough, to push them into a new level of understanding about the power of prayer. Christians have been given the authority to come before God's throne, and in Jesus' name battle the darkest elements loose in this world. We need to learn to grasp that authority. Use it. Trust it. My prayer for readers of *Dead of Night* is that they will learn to demand of themselves a victorious and vibrant prayer life, regardless of the apparent hopelessness of their situations.

Brandilyn Collins

Prologue

*N*ot so pretty in death, are you.

Head unnaturally flexed, back cruelly arched. Ugly contorted mouth, eyes wide in shock, limbs all locked tight.

Now your outside looks like your inside—a black soul, an immoral soul, a horrified and horrifying soul, bound for the black pits, the depths of darkness, for eternity, ever and ever on.

Skin still warm, clothes all askew, bleached blonde hair tangled around your devious head, with wisps caught on your evil tongue. Dead, dead, dead and gone, and who will miss you now?

Sit back and look at you, deserving the work of my hands. Look you up and down, your shoes kicked off in the convulsions, your wrists bent and fingers curled like the limbs of an arthritic tree, one knee drawn up toward your chest.

How easily and hard they fall, the proud and vain and shallow.

But. . .

Sweep aside the coarse white-yellow hair. There it is. Pretty earring. Pretty, pretty bauble, so shiny, with a big white stone and little blue stones around it, playing with the spectrum like shimmery fairies. Put my finger behind your earlobe, move it this way and that, watch the dancing colors catch the light. My earring now, only mine to keep and smile at and watch it shine.

How to take it? It is connected to your ear, right through it. Silly, arrogant woman, piercing holes in your body in the name of beauty. Like her. Self-absorbed and flirtatious, making eyes at the men, swaying hips and pouting lips, and meanwhile the child saw and was unseen, and no one else knew, and no one else cared, and who would tend the child?

Pull. Tug. Rip at the earring, and still it will not come. It latches to your ear like a leech sucks skin. You are keeping it from me, you defy me in death, you shout to me in your silence that you will not be de-jeweled, not be robbed of the sparkly outward display of your wretched and gaudy heart.

Hurry away, my footsteps scuffing the kitchen floor to grab what I need. I will cut it from you, and your yawning mouth will scream in silent agony, but no one else knows, and no one else cares, and who will tend to you?

There.

The earring is mine.

Hold it close to my eyes. Feel the hardness of the stone with my finger, tip it, turn it, watch the light play, the fading light of the setting sun. Darkness creeps toward the earth like it has crept over you, and to the ground you will now go, ashes to ashes and dust to dust, to be remembered no more, to wither and rot.

In the dead of night you will be taken. As the dead of night, so shall you ever be.

Chapter 1

Tuesday, June 21

The moment before it began, I stood in my bedroom, folding clothes.

In the last year I've developed a kind of sixth sense—a lingering smudge from my brushes with death. A sense that jerks my head up and sets my eyes roving, my ears attentive to the slightest sound. Nerves tingle at the back of my neck, then pinprickle down my arms and spine. The sensations surge through my body almost before I consciously register what caused them. Sometimes they are right; sometimes they are overreactions to mere surprise.

Experience has taught me to err on the side of caution. And with five local murders in as many months, I was already on edge.

Something . . . something downstairs . . .

My arms stopped to hover over my bed, a half-folded shirt dangling from both hands.

"Hey!"

The male voice echoed up from our great room one floor below— a voice I didn't recognize. It mixed surliness with a throaty growl, like stirred gravel.

I didn't hear the doorbell.

"Hey!" The voice again, impatient.

My thoughts flashed to Kelly, my fourteen-year-old. She'd fallen asleep down there, on one of the oversize couches near the fireplace. My daughter in a vulnerable position . . . some man I didn't know standing over her?

Kelly gasped—loudly enough for me to hear. With the expansive wooden floor and the wood wainscoting of our great room, sounds echo. The fear in that gasp jolted me into action. Almost before I knew what I was doing, I'd run for my purse on the nightstand. My fingers fumbled, looking, searching. Within seconds I felt the smooth, frightening comfort of my gun.

I yanked it out.

No time to think. Pure instinct took over. Hadn't Chetterling told me it would? I wrapped my hands around the gun, trigger finger ready, and sneak-sprinted down the hall. Below me, the great room jerked into view through banister railings. I skidded to a halt at the landing and nearly dropped the gun. My terrified eyes fixed on an unknown man in profile to me, hulking over Kelly. He was in his early twenties. Big— maybe six-two?—with vein-laden, bulging biceps. The wide nose and lips of an African American, but with dusty-colored skin. Light brown hair in thick dreadlocks. Kelly had raised up on one elbow, mouth open, her expression a freeze-frame of shock.

My legs assumed the stance Chetterling had taught me. Feet apart and planted firmly. My arms stretched before me over the banister, gun pointed at the man's head.

"Stop!"

He jerked toward me, eyes widening. Both arms raised shoulder height, large fingers spread. "Hello. Wait one minute. I was just looking for Stephen."

His cultured tone so surprised me that I almost lowered the gun. From the looks of him, I'd expected more of an urban hip-hop. *Annie, keep it together; he's right near Kelly!* I stared at him, breath shuddering. How could this be happening? I'd drawn a *gun* on someone. Someone who stood *right next* to my daughter. "Back away from her."

He retreated one step.

What if this was the man who'd killed those five women? "More."

"Would you mind putting the gun away?" He shuffled back two more steps, but he couldn't go far. Another three feet and he'd hit the armchair facing the fireplace. To his left sat a big glass-topped coffee table, to his right the sofa where Kelly lay.

Any second he could lunge for her, pull her in front of him as a shield. What would I do? *Chetterling, we never practiced anything like this!*

"Look." Sulkiness and an arrogant irritation now coated his voice. "I was just going to ask her about Stephen; you don't have to threaten my life."

My insides shook, but my hands did not waver. When I spoke, my voice carried the cynical disgust of a policeman on patrol. "I don't recall anyone letting you in the house."

"The door was unlocked."

Unlocked. Still, that was hardly an invitation. My jaw clenched. "You in the habit of just walking into people's homes?"

He shrugged.

Anger tromped up my spine. How *dare* he act so nonchalant? "Well, let me tell you something—you picked the *wrong* house to walk in to."

"So I noticed." A smirk etched his lips. "Is Stephen here?"

Kelly still had not moved. He could be upon her in a heartbeat. *God, help me! How do I get her to safety?*

"Kelly." I kept my eyes on the man. "Get up *now*. Run into my office and lock the door."

My daughter blinked, as if trying to rouse herself from a bad dream. Then she scrambled to her feet. I watched my target, the two-inch barrel Chief Special aimed at his head. A double action revolver, the gun didn't need to be cocked to fire. My finger remained poised to pull the trigger if he gave me reason.

In my peripheral, I saw Kelly back away from the man, then turn and run toward the office. She disappeared beneath the landing where I stood, her bare feet slapping against the hardwood floor. My office door banged shut. The lock clicked.

Relief flooded my chest. At least my daughter was safe. I knew she would call 911. With experiences like we've had, you don't fool around.

"All right." I forced strength into my words. "Now. Who are you?"

He flicked an impatient look at the ceiling. "Are you going to put that gun down or not?"

"I asked you a question."

Cold eyes glared at me. "Blake."

Who knew if he was telling the truth? "Blake who?"

"Smith, all right? S-m-i-t-h."

Yeah, sure. His cockiness rattled me. This was not a man who'd bow an inch for authority. I could feel sweat beading on my forehead. My only hope was that he couldn't see it. "What do you want with my son?"

His arms lowered until both hands were in front of his chest, fingers still spread. "I simply need to talk to him."

"About what?"

"Business."

Business? "Really. And what kind of business would that be?"

He stuck his tongue under his top teeth, then pulled it away with a sucking sound. "You're his mother, correct? The famous forensic artist."

The way he said those words. His insolence might as well have been a back-handed slap. If we were close enough, I'd bet anything he would jump at me, swipe the gun from my hands. My palms grew clammy. I tightened my grip on the weapon.

Blake eyed me with belligerence, then slowly lowered his left hand. He pointed his right index finger at me. "You will give Stephen a message for me."

Anger ballooned my lungs, pinned them against my chest. Now he was telling *me* what do? When he'd walked into *my* home? Stood over my sleeping, innocent daughter? My fingers began to tremble. "Get out of my house!"

"All right, all right, I'm going."

He turned his back on me, as if I posed not the slightest threat, and ambled around the far side of the coffee table like some languid lion aroused from sleep. I almost expected him to yawn. Then he took his time moving around the couch. Only then did he face me once more.

"You tell your son that Blake is looking for him, you hear? He'll know why. And you tell him this." His eyes narrowed, sharpening blades that would cut steel. "He *won't* be able to hide from me."

With a sneer, he turned and stalked away, the satiated predator from a death-spared deer.

I did not move, gun still pointed. He strode onto the porch and slammed the door.

My legs wobbled as I made my way down our wide curving staircase of polished wood. *Dear God, what now?* All the terrible murders around Redding, now this. Vaguely, I heard a car door slam outside, the squeal of tires. Fear for Stephen gripped me. What had he done this time? My seventeen-year-old son had been nothing but trouble for a couple years, this last twelve months in particular. A year ago he'd faced his first court appearance for drug possession, receiving six months' probation—which he hadn't obeyed. After that came rounds of weekend work detail, then time in juvenile hall. Lately I'd begun to suspect he was selling drugs. Where else had he gotten the new clothes, the constant stream of new CDs? His "a-friend-gave-it-to-me" explanations had long since worn thin.

I hit the bottom of the steps and ran across the long great room. Gun still in hand, I locked and bolted the front door, then peeked through our tall windows to check outside. No sign of Blake. No unknown car. For a moment I leaned against the glass, forehead on my arm, and tried to steady my breathing.

Only then did a thought cross my mind, irreverent in its timing. My sister would be so proud of me. Gun-toting Jenna's insistence that I learn to shoot had finally paid off.

Far behind me, the lock on my office door clicked.

"Mom?" Kelly's voice pinched with fear.

I veered from the window. "Yes, honey, it's okay. He's gone." The forced lightness in my tone sank like lead.

Kelly sidled from around the hall corner, hiccuping a sob. She ran toward me, hands outstretched, not even noticing that I still held a loaded gun. What to do with it? I barely had time to lay it on the windowsill before she flew against my chest and burst into tears. "Oh, Kelly, I'm so sorry." Wrapping my arms around her, I rocked her as if she were a little girl. "It's okay, now, everything's all right. He didn't really want to hurt you. He was just trying to wake you up to ask about Stephen."

Her body shook. "At first I thought . . ."

Of course she had. "I know, I know." Even though the murders had occurred on the other side of Redding, anyone in Kelly's position would have feared the same thing. All denials had ceased after the third body was found in March. A serial killer roamed the area. A killer with remarkable cunning and a chilling manner of murdering his victims.

"But who is he?" Kelly's voice hitched. "I've never seen him before, and I know a lot of Stephen's friends."

I closed my eyes. If only I could close my mind to the questions. Kelly had just finished her freshman year of high school, and Stephen, his junior year. For the first time since we'd moved to Grove Landing, they attended the same school, which had afforded Kelly an all-too-vivid knowledge of the kids Stephen hung out with. But even the worst of them couldn't measure down to this Blake Smith.

If that was his real name.

"He looked older than a high schooler to me." I rubbed Kelly's back. "That's probably why you haven't seen him."

But why was Stephen hanging around with someone like that? Someone so threatening? Only one answer came to mind: drugs.

A shiver rolled across my shoulders.

"Kelly." I kept my tone as gentle as possible. "You didn't lock the door when you came in from Erin's. I know it's hard to remember in the summer, when you two are running back and forth so much, but you really *do* need to."

"I know. I'm sorry. Believe me, I won't forget again."

I patted her back.

She pulled away to look at me, her eyes red. "I called 911. You'd better call them back—I hung up when I saw the guy drive away."

"Yeah, okay." I loosened a strand of brown hair from her cheek, struck for the millionth time by her beauty. When had my daughter grown as tall as I was? "You sure were brave, Kelly. That must have been really scary."

She blew out air and stepped away, summoning the fortitude of her fourteen years. "Yeah, scary all right. I've never seen you pull a gun on somebody."

"I meant the *man*, Kelly."

"Oh."

We managed to smile at each other.

Speaking of the gun, I needed to put it away. But first I needed to call the Shasta County Sheriff's Department. If Detective Ralph Chetterling had heard that 911 call, he'd no doubt be speeding here like a freight train. So would anyone else from the department, for that matter. With a massive hunt for a predatory killer under way, every member of local law enforcement had the jitters.

"Kelly, I need to make that call." I turned to pick up my weapon, and she flinched from it. Kelly felt the same way I did about guns—she was scared to death of them.

I headed into the kitchen for the phone, my artist's mind conjuring Blake Smith's features. The wide nose, the deep-set eyes. Thick, almost straight eyebrows. As soon as I got the chance, I would draw that face from memory. Give it to Chetterling, have him show it around the department. Maybe some deputy would know this guy. Although I wasn't sure which would be worse—if a member of law enforcement did know Blake . . . or didn't.

What had Stephen done?

I lay the gun down on the kitchen counter and picked up the phone to dial 911, my mother's heart quailing. If only I could stop the wreckage of my son's life. My call was answered on the first ring. "Hi, it's Annie Kingston."

"Annie! Are you all right, what's going on? We've got a car on the way."

"Thanks. The immediate danger is over. No need for any deputies to hurry now, but I'd still like someone to come so I can make a report."

I explained what had happened and described Blake. "The deputy coming here should keep an eye out for this guy. Unfortunately I didn't see what kind of car he was driving."

"Okay, we've got it. The unit will be there in about five minutes. Stay safe, Annie."

Yeah. Stay safe.

Back upstairs, as I placed my gun into my purse, a dark precognition swooped over me. I had driven Blake Smith out of my house, but not out of our lives. Stephen was in real trouble this time.

Not with law enforcement, but with the criminals themselves.

CHRISTY AWARD WINNER

Jack Cavanaugh
Jerry Kuiper

DEATH
WATCH

ZONDERVAN

Jack Cavanaugh

Acclaimed by critics and readers alike as a master storyteller, Jack Cavanaugh has been entertaining and inspiring his readers with a mixture of drama, humor, and biblical insight for over ten years. He lives in Southern California with his wife, Marni.

A Word From the Author

Days like 9/11 come without warning and without mercy. Sometimes it's national. Sometimes it's personal. Sometimes it's both. You wake up, and the next thing you know, your world is upside down and everything you've believed in for years is tested. *Death Watch* begins on such a day for Sydney St. James, a rookie television news reporter in Los Angeles. She goes to work thinking it's just another day. By lunch, she's involved in a mystery of death and terror that tests the very core of her Midwestern evangelical roots.

Jerry and I wanted to tell a story that would challenge readers to re-examine the public awareness of their evangelical faith. Do the people we work with really know what we believe? What we stand for? *Death Watch* is based on the concept that on any given a day a crisis can arise like a pop quiz, revealing our personal beliefs to the world. We purposely crafted a final sentence that we hope will ring like a clarion bell: "Knowing what I know now, how can I possibly keep silent?"

Jack Cavanaugh

Prologue

Delta Flight 1565, the red-eye from Atlanta to Los Angeles, was uncharacteristically on time as it descended from thirty thousand feet over a scrub-brush-dotted California desert.

The man in seat 4A opened his ultra-thin laptop and connected his cell phone to the modem port. A mouse click initiated the sequence of dial tone, keypad tones, and connection static common to accessing the Internet.

"I swear those things are gonna be the death of us," the man seated next to him said. "Between laptops and cell phones, a guy can't get a moment's peace anymore. Time was a business trip meant a nap and drinks on the plane and a girlie revue at night. Now it's spreadsheets and reports in the hotel room and email in flight." He grinned. "Not this time, pal. My hard drive crashed just before takeoff." The grin widened. "Took three 'Oops!' to crash it, too."

"What business?" 4A asked.

"Auditor. IRS." The man next to him laughed. "Yeah, that's the expression I usually get."

"Sorry. I've never met an IRS auditor."

"Lucky you."

It was the first exchange between the two men since takeoff four and a half hours earlier.

The IRS auditor sat in the aisle seat. His rumpled gray suit coat was unbuttoned, his tie loosened. He leaned back and gazed at 4A's computer screen, interested in how another man did his email.

A high-resolution image of a rotating earth filled the screen. A tiny envelope seemed to rise out of Europe. It got larger as it circled the globe. After a single orbit it filled the screen with the software company's familiar triangular logo. A female voice said, "You have thirteen new messages."

The auditor leaned closer.

"Do you mind?" 4A said.

"Oh, sorry . . ." Straightening himself in his seat, the auditor signaled to the flight attendant. "Another scotch and soda."

4A clicked on the envelope graphic. A column of file folders appeared. A digit in brackets beside each folder indicated the number of messages that had been routed into each one.

```
OFFICE          [3]    UNREAD MESSAGES
PERSONAL        [2]    UNREAD MESSAGES
ADS / SPAM      [7]    UNREAD MESSAGES
```

That left one message the program was unable to route. The email's routing data was displayed.

```
From:    <blocked by sender>
To:      Seat 4A
Sent:    Wednesday, September 25, 2005
         6:17 a.m.
Subject: Death Watch
```

Beneath it were three options:

```
Read
Save to folder
Delete
```

The man in seat 4A stared at the subject line. For a full minute he didn't breathe, neither did his heart beat. Then, pointer-icon shaking, he clicked on the Read option.

A new window opened with the text of the message.

```
You have been selected for death. Precisely
forty-eight hours from the time of this trans-
mission you will die.

This is an official Death Watch notice.
```

Seat 4A glanced nervously at the man next to him who was busy eyeballing the flight attendant as she handed him his drink.

As casually as he could, 4A clicked the program closed and eased shut his laptop with the same slow, deliberate motion a mortician would use to lower the lid of a coffin. 4A's breathing came in short, shallow gulps.

The auditor didn't seem to notice his distress. Taking a sip of his drink, the man reached for the phone that was embedded in the headrest of the seat in front of him. Balancing his drink, a phone card, and the handset, the auditor's freckled finger punched in a number. He stopped after three digits.

"What in blue blazes . . .?" Pulling the phone away from his ear, he looked at it, then listened again. To 4A, he said, "There's an incoming call! That's not possible, is it?"

Heads in the first-class section turned his direction.

The man across the aisle frowned. "Those phones can't take incoming calls."

"That's what I thought," said the auditor. "But I got an operator telling me to hold for an incoming call."

"That's impossible."

"I swear, that's what she said!"

The auditor put the phone to his ear, slowly, almost as though he expected something to jump out at him. "He . . . Hello?"

He listened for a moment.

His eyes grew wide.

He held the phone out to 4A. "It's for you."

"Me? You don't know who I am."

The IRS auditor spoke with a queer tone of voice. "She told me to hand the phone to the man in seat 4A. That's you, isn't it?"

The handset was shaking. The auditor seemed desperate to get rid of the phone. He leaned across the aisle. "It's bad news, I tell you. Believe me, I know. I've delivered it often enough."

"What did they say?"

"This woman just said to hand the phone to 4A. But she had a really weird voice. Eerie, you know? It echoed like it was coming from the bottom of a well."

"Probably just a bad connection."

A perky blonde flight attendant appeared. She spoke to 4A with a smile. "I'm sorry, sir, you'll have to hang up. We're beginning final approach."

Seat 4A held up a finger. "One moment, please." He placed the phone to his ear.

The voice offered no greeting.

You have forty-eight hours. Your Death Watch begins now. This is your second and final notification.

Then the line went dead.

Outside the double-paned window, an endless patchwork of L.A. streets, frame-houses, strip malls, and palm trees slid beneath Delta Flight 1565 in a dizzying blur.

Chapter 1

Not today! Oh please, not today!"

Sydney St. James punctuated each syllable with the heel of her hand against the steering wheel of her stationary Volvo.

A black Cadillac SUV rose up in front of her like a cliff. Behind her, an ancient white van with rust spots that looked like some form of car cancer appeared to be wedged up against her. With parked cars to the right and a stalled lane of cars to the left, she was boxed in. No one had moved in the last ten minutes.

"I can't be late. Not today!"

Her destination, KSMJ-TV, Channel 2, was within sight, so tantalizingly close it was maddening.

The worst part was, she allowed for this. She'd given herself an extra thirty minutes to make the commute from Glendale just in case traffic was bad. But predicting L.A. traffic was like predicting the weather. Patterns and forecasts were useless.

The Hollywood Freeway gobbled up the extra time and more. In a word, it was clogged. The morning radio newscasters referred to it as *congestion*. For Sydney, the word was not descriptive enough. She'd seen film footage of faster moving lava flows. She preferred *clogged*. Like a drain. Ugly, smelly, and always inconvenient.

When she finally reached her off ramp, she checked the time. It would be close, but she had a chance. At first, traffic on Sunset Boulevard was like any other morning. Sydney managed the go-and-slow with a practiced two-step on the brake and accelerator. Then she saw red, the color of every commuter's nightmare. Brake lights as far as the eye can see. Sydney's stomach twisted into a double knot.

"Why today?" she moaned. She banged the steering wheel a couple more times.

Her father had warned her it would be like this. "There's nothing out in Los Angeles but gridlock and whackos shooting at each other. Take the job in Tulsa. It's better suited to a Midwestern girl."

But her father didn't understand news broadcasting. L.A.'s television market share dwarfed Tulsa. If she could make it as a newscaster in L.A. she could have her pick of stations anywhere in the nation. Assuming, of course, she could actually get to work.

Sydney cranked down the driver's side window of her ten-year-old beige station wagon and stuck her head out to see what was causing the delay. The SUV in front of her was too wide. All she got for her effort was a lungful of exhaust and a handful of stares, first at her, then at her car.

It was a Southern California thing.

The Volvo seemed like a good idea when she bought it used two years ago in Iowa. She'd remembered hearing someone say Volvos were good, reliable cars. Solid. Safe. What really attracted her to it was the number of heaters—front, back, under the seats. Now, with Canadian cold fronts several state lines away, it didn't seem like such a big deal. She'd only used the heater twice since moving to California. Out here, people equated style with status, and a beige Volvo station wagon was better suited to a retired Swedish farmer than an ambitious young female reporter for a major television station.

She checked her watch.

The meeting would start in five minutes. Even if traffic started moving right now, by the time she parked the car and walked back to the station she'd still be late.

Helen would save the assignment for her, wouldn't she? How could she fault me for gridlock?

A voice played in Sydney's head.

"There are no excuses in journalism."

Professor Puckett. Journalism 101.

"When you're handed an assignment, you get it done. Period. No excuses. If it's getting a statement, you dog the source until you get the quote. If it's on location, you get there even if you have to grow wings and fly."

Puckett was old school, tough as leather, with an impressive broadcasting pedigree.

He told his class of journalist wannabes, "The word *deadline* was coined at Andersonville, a notorious Confederate prisoner of war camp. A peripheral wire stretched around the entire facility. Any prisoner crossing that wire was shot on sight. In journalism, time is the wire. Cross it and you're dead."

Sydney glanced anxiously around. In the movies this was where the hero jumps out of the car and makes a run for it. But then, the films where that happened were usually shot in New York. This was L.A., where *everyone* owned a car. Jumping out and making a run for it wasn't an option.

So, what were her options?

She threw the transmission into *Park*. With the engine still running, she climbed out of the car in search of options. A number of other drivers were doing the same thing. They didn't venture far, ready to jump back behind the wheel if traffic started moving. Some drivers stood in the open door, using the floorboard as a stepping stool to get a better look.

With the mountainous black Cadillac SUV blocking her view, Sydney had no choice but to venture away from her vehicle. What she saw wasn't encouraging.

The cause of the traffic tangle was a hazy blue Ford Taurus. Its hood mangled, facing oncoming traffic, it blocked the intersection of Sunset and Vine. Steam rose from under its hood as the car gave up the ghost. The back half of a policeman protruded from the driver's side window as he assisted the victim or victims. In the distance an approaching siren wailed.

Three black-and-white cruisers surrounded the wreck at odd angles, their driver-side doors standing open. Police milled about the scene, thumbs hooked in their belts, showing no concern for the long line of stranded commuters. It was obvious Sydney wasn't going anywhere anytime soon. Nobody was.

A smile surprised Sydney, prompted by the first happy thought she'd had all morning. Nobody was going anywhere! Nobody. If she was stuck in traffic, so was everyone else at the station. *Nobody* was going to make it to the meeting on time.

Then, as quickly as the smile appeared, it faded.

Standing on the far side of the intersection, preparing to cross the street, was Helen Gordon. An attractive middle-aged African-American woman, impeccably dressed in a stylish gray business suit, Helen surveyed the accident scene with a seasoned eye, then checked her watch.

Sydney didn't have to be clairvoyant to know what Helen was thinking. Five minutes to make it to the meeting. Plenty of time.

Sydney slapped the top of a white Acura in frustration.

The driver-side window of the Acura rolled down. A balding man stuck his head out. "Hey, lady! It's a car, not a drum."

"Sorry."

The man looked Sydney up and down. His anger gave way to a wolfish grin. "No problem, sweetheart. How 'bout if you join me? We can discuss payment for damages."

Without comment, Sydney retreated to her car, more desperate than ever. How was she going to convince Helen she had what it took to be a professional political correspondent if she couldn't even make it to a morning meeting?

For the last year and a half Sydney had been paying her dues, which meant taking assignments that ran the gamut from cute to sensational. Her first west coast on-the-air report was about a mother cat that suckled an orphan puppy along with her litter of seven kittens. Sydney's second story covered the birth of a baby hippopotamus at the Los Angeles Zoo.

The station liked her coverage of the stories well enough. Sol Rosenthal, the station producer, complimented her, saying she had a knack for cute—hardly the kind of comment a serious reporter wants to hear from a producer.

Part businessman, part carnival barker, Rosenthal was a corporate suit in his late twenties. Industry execs considered him to be a real comer. This was his third television station and from all appearances, he wouldn't be with KSMJ for long. Sol Rosenthal was network bound. Thin, energetic, a fast talker, there was no newsman in him. For Sol Rosenthal, exposure was king, and the way to court success was through increased ratings.

"This'll make a splash!" he cried at one assignment meeting. Sol was always looking for ways to make a splash. "How about a story on all those impotence ads? You know, the ones with that coach and the other one with that Red Cross woman's husband."

"Mike Ditka. Former Chicago Bears coach," Grant Forsythe said. "Ditka advertises Levitra. Former senator Bob Dole does the Viagra commercials."

Forsythe was the prime time evening news co-anchor, the face of KSMJ for fifteen years. He loved nothing better than to show off his fifteen years of accumulated news trivia.

Rosenthal leaned forward, elbows on the table. "Isn't there one more?"

"Cialis," Grant said, his tone smug.

"Yeah, that's it. And they don't call it impotence anymore, do they? What's it called now?"

"Erectile dysfunction." Grant beamed like a sixth grade schoolboy.

"Here's my idea. We have Sydney do the story."

Helen Gordon frowned. "Why Sydney?"

"Because it's sweeps week, Helen. A hot blonde doing a story on erectile dysfunction? It'll make a splash."

During sweeps week broadcasters use the viewership numbers to set local advertising rates for the rest of the year. Competition between stations is fierce.

Sweeps or no sweeps, Sydney didn't want to do the story. She thought Rosenthal's idea was in bad taste. Privately she told Helen as much and tried to back out of the assignment.

Helen didn't buy it.

"We all get assignments we don't like," the veteran newswoman snapped. "So stop whining and just do your job."

Helen liked Sydney.

Helen Gordon had risen through the ranks from intern to reporter to newscaster to assignment editor and knew firsthand broadcasting was a tough business, especially for a woman. It was obvious she liked Sydney too much to coddle her.

Sydney took the assignment. Once she started researching it and realized erectile dysfunction was a serious health issue, she saw its potential.

On camera, she said, "Between fifteen and thirty million men suffer from erectile dysfunction. That's nearly ten percent of the American male population. Yet, tragically, only one man in twenty will seek treatment."

Her report explored the causes of the problem: fatigue, high blood pressure, diabetes, prostate cancer surgery, and wounds that were often the result of combat. She described how the problem affects both men and their wives. She interviewed couples, keeping their identity hidden with backlighting. She encouraged viewers suffering from erectile dysfunction to seek treatment, giving them contact information for local hospitals and counselors.

Her report didn't come off as hot as Sol Rosenthal envisioned it, but the station switchboard received a surge of phone calls from community leaders, health organizations, and others who said they appreciated the professional and tactful way the station handled the sensitive topic.

Sydney's report was a sweeps success.

Rosenthal took credit for his idea paying off. The next time sweeps week rolled around, he had another idea.

"How hot would it be for Sydney to do a story on Hollywood hookers? A hot blonde interviewing hookers. It'll make a splash!"

This time Sydney didn't complain, though she did grit her teeth when Helen readily agreed Sydney was the best reporter for the job.

Sydney turned the assignment into a family issue. As the story aired, Sydney reunited a sixteen-year-old Colorado runaway, now living on the streets, with her parents.

The switchboard flooded with calls.

While Sydney was pleased with the response, she feared her success would be her undoing. Rosenthal would never see her as anything other than a feature story reporter.

Her hope lay with Helen Gordon. Helen knew her heart, and yesterday had stopped shy of promising her an assignment to interview the governor of California who was coming to L.A. to announce a get-tough-on-gangs bill. The assignment would be handed out at this morning's meeting.

All Sydney had to do was get there.

From the middle of clogged Sunset Boulevard, she shouted at the sky, "Why is this happening to me?"

An instant later, Sydney's darkening morning turned black.

Strolling up behind Helen Gordon was Cori Zahn, the station's evening co-anchor and Sydney's self-appointed nemesis. Like Helen, somehow Cori Zahn had managed to escape the traffic.

"How? How? How?" Sydney groaned. "Is there a secret underground boulevard I don't know about?"

A brunette, Cori was a competent newscaster, attractive, but not beautiful. And in an industry that worships physical appearance even above talent, she would always be threatened by beautiful, young talent. That made Sydney the enemy.

Standing beside her beige Volvo in the middle of Sunset Boulevard, Sydney watched helplessly as Helen Gordon reached the front door of KSMJ with Cori Zahn right behind her.

Cori caught up. The women exchanged pleasantries. Apparently Cori said something about the accident, because both women turned toward the intersection.

Sydney saw her chance. Raising both hands over her head, she waved and shouted, hoping to catch Helen's attention. Instead, she caught Cori's.

The two rivals exchanged glances. Just as Helen turned to see what Cori was looking at, Cori distracted her and held open the station door.

Helen entered the building. Cori followed, but not without first turning to Sydney and grinning.

With a frustrated yelp, Sydney fell back into the Volvo. She grabbed her purse and plunged her hand into it, searching for her cell phone. A moment later, she was connected to the station. Helen didn't always go to her office before the morning meeting, so Sydney left a message with the receptionist, leaving explicit instructions for the girl to see that Helen Gordon received it.

That done, Sydney slumped behind the wheel. She'd done all she could do, hadn't she?

There are no excuses. Get there if you have to grow wings.

Sydney jumped out of the car. She looked around for a pair of wings. Something. Anything that would get her in that meeting.

She spotted a couple standing on the sidewalk, gawking at the tall buildings. Pointing.

Sydney grabbed her keys from the ignition switch. This wasn't New York, but it was time to get out and run.

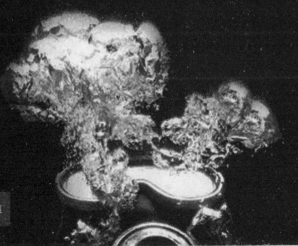

TOM MORRISEY
Author of YUCATAN DEEP

A BECK EASTON ADVENTURE

DEEP BLUE

Beck Easton's love for diving uncovers a
deeply buried secret...a deadly one.

ZONDERVAN

Tom Morrisey

Tom Morrisey is a mountaineer, aviator, shipwreck diver, and explorer, who holds a Full Cave certification from the National Speleological society—Cave Diving Section. He has launched, edited or contributed to numerous national publications and is an award-winning adventure travel writer. A popular speaker, he is also active in both youth and prison ministry. Morrisey earned an MFA in creative writing from Bowling Green State University, and his fiction has been featured in numerous anthologies and magazines. His previous novel, *Yucatan Deep*, was a 2003 finalist for the Christy Award. He and his family live in rural Jackson County, Michigan.

A Word From the Author

"Everyone has their price." We've all heard that. But what happens when you get within grasp of your price, when you actually have your hands on riches beyond your wildest imagination-and you find out they're worth nothing at all? That's the learning experience that Beck Easton has already gone through, and it's the experience he guides Jennifer Cassidy through in my romantic suspense novel *Deep Blue*, the initial volume in the Beck Easton Adventure series. What Beck helps Jennifer discover is that laying up treasures on earth is like decorating the departure lounge at the airport-the ultimate misplaced priority.

In writing *Deep Blue*, I was motivated by one deep and central truth-that we are all moving together in life's journey, but our destinations-and our reasons for traveling-differ. It is my wish that this novel moves my readers to investigate what it is they're after on their journey. For those who are living a life without Christ, I pray that this novel helps guide them to him. And for those who already know Jesus, it is my hope that they realize that they are not merely travelers on this journey. They are messengers. They are guides.

Blessings,
Tom Morrisey

PROLOGUE

Pale and leaden in the predawn light, the spring looked like nothing special, like a pond of rainwater standing in the tan limestone basin. It was only when a body got close that you saw what made it different: the surface of the water all dancing and rippling from the flow surging up from the depths, a small run draining the overflow into the tea-brown waters of the Itchetucknee.

Jonah Winslow paused, gazing at the rippling headpool, and dragged his threadbare sleeve across his forehead. The spring looked as it had when he'd first seen it, a full four decades earlier.

He shifted his burden, a Confederate Army foraging bag, thick canvas sagging with the weight of what it carried. Then he turned and looked back at the slender young woman who was picking her way among the tree roots, planting her slippered feet with care. She came to a halt beside him and her face was white in the half-light, a striking contrast to the blackness of Jonah's own, white and finely featured, like the china dolls the old slave had watched her play with as a child.

"Oh, Uncle." She shook her head and looked up at him, blue eyes wide. "Let us go home. This is far too dangerous."

"Now, child." He kept his voice low, the voice he'd used to calm her through all the hard years. "If I've done this once, I've done it a hundred times. Wasn't I just in there yesterday, getting things ready?"

Cecilia Donohue blinked and said nothing.

"Besides," Jonah said, "after tomorrow morning, we won't have a home. Carpetbagger's coming. Time to do this chore."

He set the bag at his feet and stripped off his faded chambray shirt, his chest still damp from the walk. Next, he untied the rope that he wore as a belt and stepped out of his patched cotton trousers.

Jonah Winslow made no pretense at modesty. Nor did the young woman avert her eyes. Jonah knew that Cecilia Donohue loved him like family, yet it no more upset her to see him naked than it would have to see any of her father's cattle or horses just as nature had created them. Jonah didn't blame her for this. It was how she'd been raised, who she was.

Cecilia glanced down at the forage bag.

"It will be safe here?" It wasn't the first time she'd asked.

"Yes, ma'am." Jonah Winslow turned and met her gaze, careful not to glance away as he spoke. "I wrapped it in cheesecloth. Crimped a sheet of lead foil 'round it—last sheet we had. Then I coated the whole thing with beeswax. It can lay there for years if it has to. But it won't have to."

He turned and walked down into the spring, wading deeper and gasping just a bit as he stepped off a ledge and the cool water rose to his waist. He kept going until he was shoulder deep, and then he turned and looked back at Miss Cecilia, standing there with the sky growing gray behind her.

"Hurry back, Uncle Jonah," she whispered.

"Two minutes." Jonah's throat felt thick, his words gravelly. "Won't take no longer than that, Miss Cecilia."

He turned back to face the boil of the spring and the two dark openings that gaped at the bottom of the pool. Slowly, deeply, he began to pull in great, long draughts of air.

One breath ... two ... three ...

Jonah's shoulder ached from the forage-bag strap, and he thought about the first time he'd done this, the summer of his fifteenth year, when even the work of loading an entire wagon with water barrels could do little to tire him. He and young Master Cameron, the boy who would one day be Cecilia's father, had come here in the midst of a drought to fetch water. Afterward, they'd gone swimming to escape the heat, and the young master had dared Jonah to dive down into the dark opening that yawned beneath their bare feet.

DEEP BLUE

Jonah had known what the other boy must have been thinking. Most of the plantation's slaves were deathly afraid of the springs, of the "haints" said to live there, waiting to draw swimmers to their doom.

But while Jonah had listened carefully to every circuit preacher who had ever come through and knew there was a devil and evil within the world, he also knew talk of haints was foolishness. Even so, when he'd first dived down, he no sooner touched the rim of the cave than his lungs were burning for a breath. He'd gone gasping to the surface, and the other boy's laughter had so angered him that, on the next try, he had not only gone into the cave—he had swum far back in it, found the junction that led to the other spring opening, and come rocketing out the other side.

It had been a clever trick, one that had sparked an idea with young Master Cameron. The very next Sunday, the plantation owner's son had enticed twenty neighbors to pay a nickel apiece to watch "Donohue's buck"—that was what they'd called him— perform his daredevil feat. And once they'd figured out how to prolong the excitement, Jonah and the young master had been able to coax as much as two nickels apiece from the pockets of their audience.

Four breaths . . .

The eastern sky was getting some color now, the fairest shade of pink, the sailor's color of warning. Jonah squeezed his eyes shut and resisted the urge to shake his head. *Fifty-three summers—too old for this foolishness.* He glanced back at Miss Cecilia, standing there at the spring's edge. *Known her all her life, raised her after her momma passed. I'm her only hope.*

It was a simple proposition. If the men from up North found what was in the forage bag, they'd take it. Take it and its secret and doom Miss Cecilia to a life of poverty. *Got to do it; got to hide this thing.*

Five breaths . . .

It wasn't that Jonah Winslow was afraid to die. He knew by heart the Scriptures that promised him heaven, and if heaven was better than this world for white folk, it was even more so for a man raised a slave. Master Cameron and his family had been as good to Jonah as the times would allow, but they had still treated him as property. Jonah had seen his brothers grow stooped and bent from long hours in the fields, seen his only sister sold away up to Georgia.

Six breaths ...

Jonah loved the young woman at the spring's edge like his own blood, more than that, if such a thing was possible.

Seven ...

He took this one as deeply as he could, held it, and dove for the bottom of the spring.

Springflow pushed and tugged at the fringe of Jonah's hair, the water feeling heavy around him, the weight of the forage bag pulling him down like an anchor. Shifting the bag around to the small of his back, Jonah crawled along the boulders on the bottom of the spring basin, snaking across the flats and into the dark, gaping mouth of the cave.

Pig bladders. That was the trick that had allowed Jonah to stay down so long on those two-nickel Sundays: pig bladders, like what they'd blown up to use as kick-balls when he was a boy. He and Master Cameron had pumped the bladders full with a bellows, pumped them close to bursting because the water would shrink them at depth. Then they'd tied them to window sash weights and hidden them in the caves on the morning before a dive. That gave Jonah air to breath. It let him bide his time underwater, exploring the darkness while he breathed down first one bladder and then the next.

Now, groping in the flooded blackness some forty years after he had learned that trick, Jonah found the four bladders he'd brought into the cave the evening before. He wasted no time as he untied the first one and sucked down a deep draught of air, wel-

DEEP BLUE

come even with the biting taste of the bladder on it. He gathered the rawhide thongs that held the other three bladders and struggled back into the darkness, the haversack trying to slide off his back, the sash weights bumping on the bottom, and the bladders tugging in the current like invisible, runaway kites.

It was on one of those long-ago dives, biding his time down in the underwater darkness while all the white folk waited up above in their Sunday-best, that Jonah had first found the side passage. Its entrance was low and overhung, easy to miss for a body finding his way by feel, but wide enough that he'd felt comfortable about going in. And there, ten feet back in that passage, his hands had fallen upon a flake of rock that pulled away easily, revealing a shallow, natural limestone shelf—the perfect hiding place for something small and valuable.

It was the first place he'd thought of when Miss Cecilia had come to him with her secret.

Jonah's lungs burned again for air. He let his breath go in a single whoosh, untied another bladder, and breathed it down in two deep breaths. This time, he was still hurting afterward. He thought through what he had to do, how the current would help push him back to the surface. *One breath's all I'll need ... all it'll take to get me back to the light.* He gulped down the air from the third bladder, as well.

The last bladder in tow, Jonah found the side passage, dipped under the overhang, found the slab, and moved it away from the wall. His hand landed on the ledge, and he pulled the forage bag over his head and placed it in the hiding place. Checking to make sure it stayed, he pivoted the slab back and rested his hand there for a moment. *Please, Lord, keep this safe.*

Done. That was done. Now it was time for Jonah to get himself out; he was the only man in North Florida—maybe the only man in the world—who could come back and retrieve this thing for Miss Cecilia.

Jonah kicked his way back, one hand up to find the overhang and guide himself beneath it in the dark. He felt the tug of a stronger flow—the main passage. Time to breathe the last of his air.

Jonah exhaled through his mouth and nose, feeling the bubbles whisking across his stubbled face in the darkness. He reached up to the bladder, found a rawhide thong, and pulled it down.

The bit of leather went slack in his hand.

No. His heart plummeted. *No!* He must have left the tag end long when he'd tied the slip knot to secure the bladder—and now he'd grabbed the wrong end in the blackness, pulling the knot free.

Arms flailing, Jonah groped with both hands in the jet-black water, but he knew it was useless. The current would have the bladder thirty feet down the passage by now.

Fighting panic, empty lungs screaming for a breath, he kicked out into the flow and swam for all he was worth—kicking and clawing for the cave entrance and the sweet summer air just beyond.

Oh, Lord. Oh, please. Please, sweet Jesus. Just get me there ... the entrance.

With nothing in his lungs, Jonah's lean body sank, bumping the stone and clay bottom of the passage. He scrabbled, floated up, and then sank again.

Keep going. Can make it. He urged himself forward. Heavy as he felt, the current had the power to flush him from the cave mouth and back to the surface. Red dots, flaming blossoms of color, swarmed before his eyes.

His lungs screamed for air.

Little bit more ... not far ... not far at all ...

He saw traces of light now, tinges of purple and rose on the rough, scalloped wall of the passage. *Gettin' there. Close.* He gritted his teeth, stifled the urge to breathe. He could already picture himself crawling out of the headpool like a half-drowned muskrat, Miss Cecilia *tsk*-ing over him, and weeping; telling him he shouldn't have tried, both of them weeping and happy.

DEEP BLUE

Then there was the whisper of a touch, like a tentacle, at his ankle. It went tight, ensnaring him. Gripped fast, he stopped, the outflow rushing all around his naked body in the gloom. *No! Ain't no haint in this cave. Ain't no . . .*

Jonah tugged again and felt something thin cutting into the skin above his ankle. He stifled a scream, and water seeped past his clenched teeth. He probed along his leg for the snare that held him fast.

One of his discarded air bladders must have lodged in a rock or a crack, and a loop of floating rawhide thong had snagged him. He gripped it with both hands, yanked with the full strength of fear, and pulled free. His foot was still caught in the cord, but the bladder and its attached weight were moving with him now, drifting down the center of the passage. He reached down for the cord, then shook his head.

Don't go messing with that now. Tend to it later. Got to get out. Already his vision was darkening; dizziness was creeping in on him. The sash weights bumped along below him, the deflated bladder catching and rolling rocks on the passage floor. His chest muscles rippled as they tried vainly to draw in . . . something. *Anything.*

He turned a corner. Ahead, dimly, he could see the entrance to the cave, a purple sky gleaming through the darkness.

His throat throbbed now as he tried to gulp down air that simply wasn't there. He bit his lips and thick blood spread across his tongue. The entrance loomed before him, close—so close that one good kick would see him through.

Jonah pushed, and the surface of the headpool roiled not twenty feet above his head. Treetops beckoned through an oval window of clear water: treetops and clouds and a dawn-pink eastern sky.

He sprang for the light—and stopped short.

Jonah tried once more, but again his leg was tethered. He reached down and yanked with both hands, but all he did was pull his body down. A waterlogged tree limb and chunks of limestone lay at the foot of the cave entrance, and one of the sash weights he was dragging had lodged there. It was stuck, wedged deep, down between two huge rocks. And it held him fast, like a man clapped in irons.

Jonah pulled again, but it was no good; he was weak as a kitten now. He reached down to free himself, but the outflow of the cave, strongest in the closeness of the entrance, blasted his arms up, high above his head. Then it kept him that way, like a man shouting "hallelujah" in a church.

Jonah's clenched teeth slacked, and water coursed into his nose and mouth. He swallowed, and spring water, so sweet on the hot days of summer, burned like molten metal in his throat. He tried to scream, but nothing came out—only the tiniest of bubbles that wobbled up and around the little sunfish darting in the clear water above him.

The sun, big and bold and blood-red, had risen. A shaft of crimson sunlight speared through the water and reached Jonah Winslow's face.

He was sad now. Sad that he had ever taken Cameron Donohue's teenage dare. Sad that he had ever gotten up the nerve to explore the flooded cave and its darkness. Sad that he had come here, a weakened, old, work-broken man, to try and do something that would have tested a young man in his prime.

But mostly, Jonah was sad about Miss Cecilia, waiting up there, not fifty feet away. He had failed her, left her all alone in a world for which she had not been prepared.

Tears flooded his eyes and melted into the cool, fresh flow of the spring. Then the first ribbons of water trickled into his lungs, and he felt the joy of release, the bright, expectant warmth of homecoming.

His eyes went wide as the sunlight flared yellow and the head-pool dissolved into blackness.

DEEP BLUE

BOOK ONE

TWIN SPRINGS

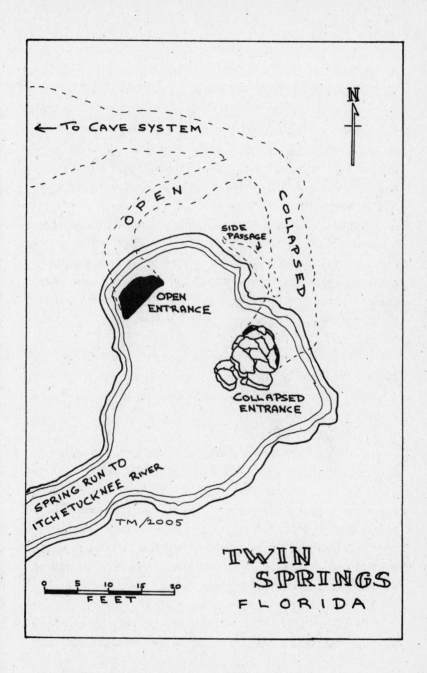

← TO CAVE SYSTEM

N

OPEN

COLLAPSED

SIDE PASSAGE

OPEN ENTRANCE

COLLAPSED ENTRANCE

SPRING RUN TO ITCHETUCKNEE RIVER

TM/2005

0 5 10 15 20
FEET

TWIN SPRINGS
FLORIDA

CHAPTER ONE

The single-story house was plain and pale yellow, about as architecturally distant from a Miami-Beach art deco as one could imagine. The vegetation across the road was pulp pines, not palm trees, and there was no beach littered with bronzed bodies. In fact, there was no beach, and no body, at all.

Jennifer Cassidy had been to Florida before—she'd come here for spring break at the insistence of a persuasive college roommate. But this nondescript house, sitting alone on a minimally landscaped lot, didn't offer a hint of the glitz and glamour she'd come to associate with the Sunshine State. In fact, were it not for the Bermuda-grass lawn and the palmettos planted along the drive, it wouldn't have appeared Southern at all.

Jennifer slowly drove the fifty yards of concrete driveway and stopped the rental car in front of a detached garage. She moved the shifter to "park," turned the rearview mirror her way, and took a quick glance.

She looked . . . efficient.

Her blonde hair was cut short, short and tufting every which way in a responsible sort of punked-out style. She twisted the mirror down, and her eyes, clear and vibrant blue—the kind of blue that made people ask if she wore colored contacts—peered back at her. The rest of her face had that no-makeup look, like the face of somebody who'd gotten up while it was still dark out, made the thirty-five-minute drive to Detroit Metro Airport in something more like twenty, and had still only barely caught her flight.

All of which was absolutely true.

This was no time for the full treatment. She dug the essentials out of her purse and made two quick passes with her blush and just the barest hint of mascara. But that still looked too unfinished, so she got out her lipstick, squinted at the mirror, and applied two smooth, stay-between-the-lines strokes. Then she finished the job with a soft-chomp on a napkin fished from her Burger King bag.

The face in the mirror still looked efficient, younger than her twenty-four years, and vaguely boyish, mostly because of the hair—what there was of it. She turned the mirror back to where it was supposed to be and put her makeup away. On the journey to "beautiful," "cute" was about as far as she'd ever gotten, and she'd learned to comfort herself with the sentiment that things could be worse. She turned the key, silencing the engine, and then rummaged in her bookbag for the webpage she'd printed out back in Ann Arbor; the address was the same as the number on the eave of the garage. This had to be the place.

Jennifer opened the car door and grimaced at the heat. *Okay, maybe I am in Florida, after all.* But it sure wasn't the Florida they put in the tourist brochures. The largest body of water she'd seen on the drive down from the airport was the Suwannee River. And the landscape had consisted mostly of stands of scrawny pine trees and open fields dotted with cattle—not the polled Herefords she'd grown up with on the farm in Ohio, but scrawny, humped and wattled creatures that looked as if they belonged in India.

The yard was quiet; no breeze. Just a few birds, probably asking one another for sunscreen. Slipping on her sunglasses, Jennifer took note of a sign that said "SHOP," and followed the paved walk around the side of the house.

Then she stopped in midstep and wished she'd spent more time with her makeup.

Because there was a man seated at a table on the brick patio, and he wasn't just any man.

This guy was a hunk: nice, strong profile, good jaw, and a head of brown hair that was just coming due for a cut and going light at the ends from the sun. He was wearing khaki shorts, aviator sunglasses, and a faded blue T-shirt that fit snugly enough to show that he was in shape and then some. His arms, tanned and garnished with blonding hair, looked almost too muscular for the tiny, bent-nose pliers in his hand. He looked older than Jennifer, but not much. She guessed that he was in his thirties, early to mid.

Probably early.

He was working on something with black rubber hoses and shiny metal fittings. It looked like a piece of scuba gear, one of those things divers used to get air from a tank. Jennifer searched for the word ... *regulator*. He was working on a scuba regulator.

"I'll be with you in a second," he said without looking up. "I'm at one of those points in this rebuild where you have to hold your tongue just right ..." He tinkered with the device for the better part of a minute, and then he set it aside and stood, wiping his hands on a shop towel. "Sorry about that. I'm Beck Easton. Call me Beck."

"Jennifer. Uh, Cassidy."

They shook hands and Easton stepped back, giving Jennifer a long, slow look from head to toe—long enough to take her from flattered to mildly irritated.

"Let's see," he said. "Five-two?"

"And a half."

"And what? A hundred and fifteen pounds?"

Jennifer lifted her chin. "A hundred and fourteen, actually."

Easton nodded and walked around to her side. "Good tone. Do you run? Work out?"

"I bike a lot, swim when I can." Jennifer considered a quick sprint back to the car.

"That's great. Strong leg muscles help. We can put a 104 on you for the intro section and go to steel 72s, maybe even 95s for the Full-Cave."

"Huh?"

"Not that you have to do it all in one shot," Easton told her, hand up. "Take your time. Work your skills between courses. Do you have your C-card and logbook with you?"

"My what?"

"Your certification card and logbook."

Jennifer removed her sunglasses and squinted. "My certification card certifying what?"

Easton cocked his head and looked at her. "Well, that you're a trained diver, of course."

"Oh. I'm not. You see ... that's why I'm here."

He removed his own sunglasses. Green eyes—nice. "I'm sorry. You want open-water lessons, then? I can do that, but I've got to tell you, a group class down at Ginnie Springs will be a lot cheaper ..."

"No." Jennifer waved her hands and cut him off. "No—I'm not here to learn to dive. I'm here to hire you to do some diving for me."

"Research diving?"

"Exactly." In fact, that was all she wanted him to put on the credit-card receipt. One word: "Research."

"Well, sure." Easton nodded. "I do some of that. Although I've got to tell you, for hydrology, things like that, there's better people. What sort of research do you have in mind?"

"I need you to find something."

Easton rubbed his nose, crossed his arms. "Find what?"

"I ... I don't know."

Easton looked at her in silence. When he spoke again, his voice was low. "Can I ask how you found me?"

"Well, I did a Google search on 'cave diving' and 'Live Oak,' and found an equipment company called Dive-Rite. When I called there, I talked to a man named Lamar, and told him I needed a good diver who won't blab what I'm doing. He said I should come see you."

"O-kay ..." Easton smiled, just a bit, and glanced at the patio table. "Here, let me get this stuff out of our way. Can I get you something to drink?"

"Sure." Jennifer grinned. *Man—is this guy good-looking.* "That'd be great. Would you have a beer?"

DEEP BLUE

Easton shook his head. "Soaking suds and blowing bubbles doesn't mix," he told her, tapping on the regulator. "I've got Coke, Diet Pepsi, root beer, and I think maybe even some Dr Pepper—had some locals diving with me last week. Or I've got some iced tea that I just made up. But I've got to warn you—it's sweet."

She grinned even more. "Sweet tea's fine."

"Great. Grab a seat. Facilities are in the shop if you need 'em."

The tea was still a little warm, so Easton heaped two heavy glass tumblers full of ice, added a stout wedge of lemon to each one—he never had figured out what good it did to slide a wafer of lemon onto the rim of a glass—and poured the tea in, the ice crackling as he did it. A car door slammed out in the driveway as he did this, and when he slid open the door to return to the patio, he saw why: his visitor now had a large black-nylon catalog case next to her and was removing thick file folders from it.

"Looks like this is going to get involved." He set a glass on a paper napkin in front of her and took a seat on the opposite side of the table.

"Well, it's ... complicated." The young woman took a sip of tea and smiled her approval. "Where do you want me to start?"

Easton glanced at the sky. "Plenty of daylight left. Start at the beginning."

"Okay." Jennifer wiped a bead of condensation off her glass and then looked up at Easton. "I'm a graduate student at the University of Michigan, the School of Information Science."

"Like IT—information technology?"

"That's part of it." She grimaced just a little as she said it. "But information science deals more with application than infrastructure. It's about sleuthing out facts, finding where the information is hiding."

"Like being a detective."

"More like a librarian." Jennifer laughed. "Sometimes both. Anyhow, I'm a second-year MS candidate, but this is my first year at U of M; I transferred in from Case Western. That put me low on the totem pole for any kind of assistantship work over the summer, but I was trying anyway—so I could keep my apartment and, you know—avoid going home and waiting tables in Wapakoneta."

Easton nodded and wondered if she was going to ramble. True, female customers at a cave-diving operation were few and far between, and this one was cute as the proverbial button, but he preferred to deal with people who could get to the point.

"Anyhow, it was starting to look as if that was just what I was going to be doing. But then my department head called me in, and there was this attorney in his office, looking for research help." She handed Easton a business card:

LOUIS F. SCARVANO
Attorney at Law
SCARVANO, MARTOIA AND WOODWARD, LLC.
1 Peachtree Centre—Ste. 3459, Atlanta, GA 30309

"I know the address." Easton handed the card back. "High-rent. I'd expect that anyone who hangs a shingle there could afford to keep his own paralegals on staff."

"He can and he does. But he didn't need legal research. He needed a family history."

"He traveled to Michigan to have you do his family tree?"

Jennifer shook her head. "Not *his* family history ..." She pulled a glossy photograph out of an envelope and handed it across to Easton. "... Hers."

Easton took a look and straightened up just a bit. The picture was obviously a copy of a much older image. Yet even rendered in shades of gray, and partly obscured by creases, the woman in the image was a stunning, raven-haired beauty with eyes that seemed to reach out and lock with his.

DEEP BLUE

"Who am I looking at?"

"Cecilia Sinclair, although she was still Cecilia Donohue when that picture was taken. Daughter of Cameron Donohue, who owned a plantation near Branford. That's near here, right?"

"About half an hour away."

Jennifer returned the photo to its envelope. "That was shot the day they announced her engagement to Augustus Baxter—"

Easton shook his head. "You said her married name was 'Sinclair.'"

"Henry John Sinclair was her second husband, originally from Baltimore, although he and Cecilia moved to Ann Arbor after the war. That's why Mr. Scarvano came to U of M for his research; Cecilia Sinclair's personal documents are kept in the archive library there, and you need a stack pass to access them."

Easton nodded. This was making sense. "And you, being a grad student, have a pass."

"Exactimundo. Cecilia's first husband was originally from Georgia."

"So that's the Scarvano connection—his client is from Georgia, one of Baxter's descendants?"

Jennifer's face went to something that was halfway between a grimace and a scowl. "I asked him, and he wouldn't say—attorney-client privilege."

Easton nodded for her to go on.

"Anyhow, Augustus Baxter's father was a plantation owner, like Cecilia's, and apparently that's how they met; their fathers knew one another; Baxter was invited to Cecilia's cotillion—her coming-out ball—chemistry happened and they got engaged. Baxter even took a job at a bank in Jacksonville, to be nearer to Cecilia. They were only engaged three months, which would have been scandalous back then, except for the fact that this was 1861. Florida had already seceded from the Union, and Baxter had accepted a commission as a captain with the First Florida Cavalry. There were a lot of hurry-up weddings down here that year."

"You seem to know a lot about the period."

Jennifer smiled. "I was a dual-major undergrad—English and history. And I've always been interested in the Civil War. Not so much the battles, but the culture. How it affected people."

She took a sip of her tea. "Cecilia was a diarist, and she wrote every day, even when paper got scarce during the war. I read her journal—pretty sad story. Her father was in the war as well, and he got injured, came home, lingered, and eventually died of his wounds. Then Augustus Baxter was killed outright in a skirmish in Virginia, and that left Cecilia alone to run a plantation that was drowning in debt and hadn't cleared a dime in more than four years."

"So she lost it to banks up North?"

Jennifer nodded. "You've got it. Northern banks bought up the loans from failing banks down here. Then the banks up north hired traveling agents who went around selling off estates, liquidating the assets. And that's what happened with Cecilia. They swooped down and sold her home right out from under her."

Easton took a sip of his own tea, lemony and sweet and satisfying. He couldn't believe he'd grown up drinking it plain. "So where does Sinclair come in?"

"I don't know." Jennifer frowned. "In the journals that I have, August of 1865 shows her destitute and scraping for a living. That's how that volume ends. Yet when the next one starts, it's later in the same year—1865—and she's up in Michigan, happily married, comfortable and living on an apple farm. That's one of the mysteries."

"One?" Easton shifted in his chair. "There's more?"

Jennifer nodded, eyebrows up.

"There's a big one." She opened a thick three-ring binder and leafed through photocopies of pages covered with a refined and feminine handwriting. She stopped, read a little, and tapped the page. "On the night before their wedding, Baxter is staying down here, at the Donohue plantation. He comes to Cecilia after dinner and tells her something. In fact, she says that by the time they get done, it's midnight. She doesn't record exactly what it is that Baxter tells her, only that it is a secret important both to them and to their country—which was the Confederacy at the time—and that he is entrusting it to her in case something happens to him after the war."

Easton looked at the binder. It had to be a good three inches thick. "And she doesn't say any more about it in all of that?"

"I think she was so concerned that she was afraid to even mention it in her own journals," Jennifer told him. "In fact, she doesn't bring it up again until it's pretty clear that the South's goose is cooked." She leafed to a section near the back of the binder. "When she gets the news of Lee's surrender at Appomattox, she wonders if 'our Secret may yet save us.' And a few months later, when the war officially ends, she wonders 'what may become of our great Secret, for which so many lives were given, and if it has not yet saved our nation, may it perhaps save us?' Meaning herself and a freed slave she calls 'Uncle Jonah,' who was the only other person left on the plantation at that point. And then she mentions it one more time."

"Which is?"

Jennifer leafed to the last few photocopied pages. "August 6, 1865—Cecilia's just about at the end of her rope. The house has been all but emptied: furniture, paintings, even any clothes of value. And now she's two days away from having to leave the house itself. She's kept this secret, whatever it was, hidden throughout four years of war. Now she's about to be cast—well, she doesn't know where. And she doesn't see how she can keep the secret safe anymore, so she confides in the only friend she has left: the former slave, Jonah. And she adds in a postscript that Jonah has come up with a plan that gives her hope."

Easton tapped the table. "But she doesn't say what it is. Am I right?"

Jennifer glanced up from her binder. "You are. Cecilia's sick with worry. Too afraid to even confide in her diary, for fear that somebody might find it in the days to come. But the next day, she has no such worries. Jonah is dead, drowned in an underwater cave where he was hiding whatever it was. He was trying to breathe off these ... like sacks of air that he took down with him. And something went wrong. He drowned. So now Cecilia's last friend is dead, the secret is gone, and she has no way of getting to it. She closes with, 'All is lost and I am alone.'"

Easton leaned forward and looked at the binder. "And that's where it ends?"

"That's where this volume ends." Jennifer closed the binder. "As I said, when the next one starts, it's Christmas of that same year, and she's married and living on the farm in Michigan."

"Poor farmers or rich?"

Jennifer frowned at the material on the table. "I'd have to say very rich. When Cecilia died in 1931, she left a lot of money to charity—half a million each to the drama departments at U of M and Eastern Michigan University, more than a million, all total, to various missions organizations. She even left eight hundred thousand dollars in trust to help restore Ford's Theater. Pretty odd for a daughter of the Confederacy, but I guess she decided it was time to bury the hatchet. She didn't have any heirs—she and Sinclair had a son, but he died in a streetcar accident in Chicago in 1893. And Sinclair himself had died years earlier, in a shipwreck on the Great Lakes in ..." Jennifer checked her notes. " ... 1868."

"So Sinclair—did he come from money?"

"I don't know. His Bible—not a family Bible, but the one he carried—is with the papers that were left with the university, and it has lots of marginal notes in it. Looks like he memorized verses, kept notes on what he was working on. But the only personal information I can find in that is their wedding date: October 14, 1865. And the first public record I've found of him is in the social pages of the *Ann Arbor Beacon* in November, announcing that they've set up housekeeping and are receiving visitors."

She paused, her shoulders sagging a bit as she looked at Easton. "You think they came back and got it, don't you? Got the money, or jewels, or the deed or whatever it was, cashed it in and went up to start a farm in Michigan ... a hundred and forty years ago."

"It's sounding like it." Easton reached over and tapped the binder. "Does it say in here what spring they used as their hiding place?"

Jennifer searched the binder and read for a moment. "Here it is. Cecilia only mentions the name one time: Twin Springs."

Easton sat back in his chair.

"What?"

"Well ..." Easton put his hands atop his head, fingers knit. "It's sounding even more like it. There are springs down here that aren't often dived, but Twin's not one of them." He wondered why a researcher wouldn't have caught this, and then shook it away. The world of cave-diving was so closed that you'd almost have to be part of it to be privy to the information. "It's on private property, but even so, over the years there've probably been two, three hundred divers through that spring and the system behind it. If anything is down there to be found, I've got to think they would have found it by now."

Jennifer Cassidy looked as if someone had pulled the plug on her. She rubbed her forehead, reached for her tea, and looked absently at the empty glass.

"Here. Let me freshen that."

Easton picked up both glasses and headed back into the house. He glanced out the window at Jennifer, chin on her palm, the picture of defeat. All of his life, he'd thought of himself as a "ready, aim ... fire" sort of person. But Jennifer Cassidy seemed like more of a "ready, fire ... aim"—the sort he'd long since learned to avoid.

So why was it that he felt so badly for her and wanted to find some way to give her hope?

He wasn't sure. But as he was filling the second glass, he remembered something that might let him do just that.

When Easton reappeared from the house, a fresh glass of tea in each hand, he was smiling. Not just smiling—grinning.

Jennifer scowled just a bit. *The cave-diving business must do pretty well. Here this guy has just talked himself out of a job, and he looks happy as a clam.* Finally, her ire got the better of her. "So what's got you so cheerful?"

"Twin Springs," he said, still smiling as he handed Jennifer her glass. "It isn't 'twin springs.' Not really. There's only one aperture—one way into the cave system. There used to be another spring head; you can see where it was and still feel some flow coming out of it. But it's collapsed—the entrance and a fair amount of passage behind it."

"And that's good because—?"

"Because the passage didn't collapse until sometime in the 1890s."

"Are you sure?" Jennifer straightened up a bit.

"Positive." Beck sat down, ignoring the drink in front of him. "As I said, Twin Springs is on private property. And most times, you take what a landowner tells you with a grain of salt. I mean, people tell you they have a 'spring' on their land, and, half the time, you go out to see it and it's not a spring at all. It's usually a sinkhole, no water coming out. But the guy that owns Twin Springs? The land's been in his family for more than a century; they probably picked it up from whatever bank it was that seized it from your Southern belle, there. And because Twin Springs was once obviously two springs, I once asked the owner if he knew what happened to the second one."

"Did he?"

"He did." Easton looked straight at her. "It was dynamited."

DEEP BLUE

Jennifer lifted her head a bit. "Why would somebody want to blow up a spring?"

"To relieve boredom, I guess. Back in the 1890s, there was even less to do around here than there is now. The locals' idea of a good time on a Sunday afternoon was to head out to a spring with a picnic lunch and a barrel of beer. And then, for after-dinner entertainment, they'd chuck sticks of dynamite into the water, watch it geyser up. Only a matter of time before somebody made a lucky shot, landed their stick in the aperture, and the explosion collapsed the cave."

"So there's a fifty-percent chance that what I'm looking for is behind all that rock?"

"I wouldn't go counting your chickens just yet." Despite what he'd just said, Easton leaned forward, one arm on the table, obviously warming up to the idea. "But you can tell, even today, that the second aperture—the one that they blew—was once much larger than the first."

Jennifer waited for a moment, then asked, "And that's important because . . . ?"

"Because of something called Bernoulli's Principle." Easton held up both hands, the fingers of his left in a tight circle, the fingers of his right touching loosely. "If you figure that the same cave system is feeding both apertures, and one is smaller than the other, the water coming out of the smaller one will have to accelerate to balance the flow. It's the same thing that happens when you turn a shower head from a coarse to a fine setting—it sprays harder, because the flow is coming through a smaller opening."

"Okay." Jennifer nodded slowly. "I follow that. But why would that mean that the larger opening is the one we want?"

"Because . . ." Easton's grin grew larger ". . . if I were diving in that cave on a breath-hold, I'd want to go against the lowest resistance possible on the way in."

Jennifer could actually feel her eyebrows rise. "The one that was collapsed."

"In the 1890s." Easton nodded twice. "They had diving suits back then, but I've never heard of anyone using one in a spring. Scuba wasn't invented until the Second World War. And the exploration of these cave systems around here didn't really get going until the sixties. Yeah, if your information is right—and if this secret, whatever it is, is waterproof—I'd say there's a chance that whatever your man put in the cave is still in there."

They sat back, looking at one another. In the distance, some bird asked another about sunscreen.

"Where are you staying?" Easton asked.

"I haven't gotten around to finding a place yet."

He laughed. "You really planned this out, didn't you?" He stood up and reached for her catalog case. "I've got a bunkhouse built onto the other end of the shop for people taking lessons. Nobody's in there right now. Let's get you settled. We can dive in the morning."

THE *Eden* HALL SERIES

THE *Lady* OF THE HALL

Author of *Eden Hall*

ZONDERVAN

VERONICA HELEY

Veronica Heley

Veronica Heley has published more than fifty books, including crime fiction, historical, and children's titles. She is currently involved in the Ellie Quicke series of crime stories and a variety of other projects. A full-time writer, she has been married to a London probation officer since 1965 and has one musician daughter.

A Word From the Author

No one's perfect. Not even me. Well, especially not me.

I don't write about perfect people because I don't know any. I write about people like myself who are exposed to worldly values all the time. I live in a big city. Some of my friends go to church, but many don't. I write about people like myself who do their best to be salt and light in the world, knowing they often fall short of what they hope to achieve, but relying on God's help to do better in the future.

For a long time I worried about whether God could really love me with all my faults. Writing *Eden Hall* helped me to explore this. In the next book in the series—*Lady of the Hall*—I found myself writing about the age-old dilemma; how can I forgive someone when I've been deeply wronged, the sinner is not sorry for what he's done, and still has the power to hurt me? Then again, how do I make the best use of the talents God has given me? These two themes are central to the continuing love story of Minty and Patrick . . . and there's more to come.

Veronica Heley

Chapter One

It was a cry for help. "Barr's in trouble. In the library. Oh, do come, quickly!"

The great house lay quiet about them. Waiting. Watchful.

Minty was fond of Barr, and couldn't refuse to help. "Of course I'll come."

The two girls passed swiftly back through the silent rooms, switching off lights as they went. When they reached the library, one girl stepped back to guard the door.

Shadows stole down from the ceiling and darkened the corners of the room.

It was a trap. Barr wasn't there. Instead there was the man Minty feared most in the world. He said, "At long, long last."

Minty balanced on her toes. "Do you really mean to rape me?"

"Who said anything about rape? You're going to come to me willingly, my lovely girl. I suppose you'll put up a token defence, but we both know that's just for show. Don't fight too hard, or I may well have to mark your face. I'm going to teach you enough so you won't want to marry anyone but me."

He lunged at her and she darted around the desk.

She felt her self-control slip and screamed. There was a listening silence. Nothing happened.

He laughed. He darted around the desk and caught her from behind as she fled. "Stop struggling, you little fool!"

He was holding her fast from behind, with both arms clamped to her sides.

She breathed rapidly, trying to snatch back her self-control. She was helpless. She couldn't do anything to save herself.

"There, now! You see, it's all going to be so easy."

Araminta Cardale—known as Minty—jumped out of bed and ran to throw back the curtains. Kneeling on the window seat, she lifted the thick, fair hair from her neck and tossed it back around her shoulders.

Two storeys below her window, a great swathe of lawn sloped down to a man-made lake. On this late September morning the water—and the Park beyond—shimmered through mist.

The sun tipped up over the horizon, bringing a flush of colour to the world. The mist over the lake thinned and parted. There hadn't been a hard frost yet, so only the topmost leaves of the trees in the Park were touched with gold.

The lawns sparkled as the first rays of the sun reached them. The sky was pale blue, washed clean by heavy dew, with not a cloud in sight.

Did all this really belong to her now? And her own true love Patrick, too? *Oh, Patrick! Are you out of bed yet? Is it too early to ring you?*

There was no photograph of him by her bedside. She grinned, thinking how he'd react if she wanted to take a photo of him.

He'd say, "Do you want to break the camera?"

Ah well; Patrick Sands wasn't anyone's idea of a pretty boy—his nose was too long for that—but he was tall, dark and elegant, and completely unaware how attractive he was to the opposite sex. He was a good man, though he'd have been embarrassed if anyone had said so, and Minty loved him as she'd never loved anyone before.

So many childhood sweethearts never find one another again. Thank You, Lord, for bringing us together again.

Yesterday she'd started the day as a poor relation and ended up as mistress of the vast Eden Hall, its surrounding acres of land and the village at its gates. Patrick had said she could do better than marry a poor country solicitor, but she'd refused to listen and now they were engaged.

She wanted to turn cartwheels. She shouted, "Yes!" and punched the air. She looked over her shoulder as if her aunt had scolded her for shouting. Then laughed aloud. Aunt Agnes belonged to the past and had no more power to hurt her.

Excitement made Minty restless. She longed to explore, and why shouldn't she? The Hall was now hers, at least till noon when it would be opened to the public and tourists would start to trickle through the State Rooms.

Well, there were certain parts which were off limits, occupied as they were for the time being by her father's second wife Lisa and her children, but she could avoid them. Below her the great house slept. Minty had the odd fancy that she could waken it to life again by visiting every room. Like Sleeping Beauty in reverse, she thought, smiling.

When Sir Micah's second wife Lisa had decided to open the Hall to the public, Sir Micah had reserved the top floor of the south wing for himself, bringing in a designer to furnish and decorate his suite. These were now Minty's own rooms. Unfortunately Minty's father had gone for the traditional-in-brocade look and the result—to Minty's mind—was a showpiece: stiff, dated and not particularly comfortable.

Her father had left Minty a great deal of money, so wouldn't it be possible to turn Eden Hall back again into a family home?

She glanced at the cheap watch she was wearing. She must keep an eye on the time, because she did have one important engagement that morning. Sir Micah Cardale had been an international financier who'd poured money into the Hall during his marriage to Minty's mother. That first marriage had led to tragedy, but Sir Micah had always been fond of Eden Hall and used it as his base in Britain, even during his later years when he'd been setting up a national charity for educational projects in deprived areas. In all his financial dealings Sir Micah had relied on a competent middle-aged woman called Annie Phillips.

Annie Phillips had been kind to the penniless Minty when she'd returned to the Hall a month ago. Annie had helped Minty to see her dying father, had found her a place to live in the village and a part-time job. Minty might now be mistress of the Hall, but she was grateful to the older woman and somewhat in awe of her. Ms Phillips had asked to see Minty at eleven, so she must keep an eye on the time. Until then she could do what she liked.

Minty pulled on a blue sweater, jeans and trainers. She didn't have many clothes and those she had were nearly all from charity shops. Autumn was coming and she'd need to buy some more. This time they would be brand new. Wowee!

Suddenly she felt hungry. There was no sign of her father's housekeeper, Serafina, who slept at the back of the suite, so Minty raided the kitchen for a chunk of bread and jam and a mug of coffee.

First things first. She would start her day and her new life with God in the Eden family chapel.

She slipped out of the door at the end of her father's suite into the tower . . . and came face-to-face with her stepbrother, Simon.

Despite herself, she recoiled. He was the last person she wanted to meet, especially in such an isolated place. He was Lisa's son from a previous marriage. And it was Lisa—previously Sir Micah's secretary—whose lies had led to the death of Minty's mother. In a shockingly short time Lisa had become his second wife and he'd adopted Simon.

Thoroughly spoilt, Simon was always in debt. He'd assumed he'd inherit everything, and had been furious when he'd learned the property was entailed on Minty. He hadn't given up; first he'd tried to seduce her, and then offered marriage. When that had failed, he'd organised attempts on her life.

Simon moved in close. "Dearest not-quite-sister, I was just coming to find you. We must talk, you and I."

His face was that of an angel, his eyes as blue as hers, his hair as fair. All the Edens were fair and blue-eyed but Simon was not an Eden, and there was a twist to his mind that came from his mother Lisa, and not from the straight-forward Edens.

Minty knew better than to trust him. Her heart was beating too fast. They were all alone in the tower. Even if she cried out for help, no one would hear. He was so close she could smell his aftershave and feel the warmth of his body.

He ran his fingertip down her cheek. "Loosen up."

She blurted out, "Patrick Sands has asked me to marry him and I've accepted."

His eyes deepened in colour and the lines of his mouth hardened. "You marry me, or no one. Understood?" He bent and kissed her, hard. He'd moved so quickly that she was taken by surprise. "There," he said, smiling again, very sure of himself. "Can your lukewarm lover match that?"

"How dare you!"

"Or else? There's no one here but . . ."

The door from the chapel clicked open and there stood her father's housekeeper, Serafina, in a quilted dressing gown, with her grey-streaked black hair in a long plait over her shoulder. Serafina folded her arms and looked at Simon as if he were a bottle of milk that had gone off.

Simon released Minty. "Another time." He ran lightly down the stairs.

"Thank you, Serafina." Minty drew in a deep breath. Despite her pretence of calmness, she was trembling. "Simon doesn't understand the meaning of the word 'no', does he?"

She went into the chapel and leaned against the door, telling herself that it was useless to get upset. Simon might think what he liked. It didn't mean it was going to happen.

Eden Hall had been built in a square around the Fountain Courtyard. To solve the problem of the wings having been built at different times and on different levels, a tower containing a staircase had been built at each corner. The top of this particular tower housed the chapel which had always been a place of refuge for the Eden women—not least for Minty's own mother through her short-lived marriage to Sir Micah. The chapel had windows on three sides and this morning was glowing with the light of the rising sun. It had a calming influence.

The white Michaelmas daisies Minty had placed there yesterday still looked fresh. She'd chosen daisies in memory of her unhappy mother and of the pact she and Patrick had made as children.

Patrick, aged ten, had been showing Minty how to make a daisy chain. She liked him better than anyone else in the whole world, except her mother and father. Patrick was an only child, like her. He'd taught her to read and write.

Minty, nearly five years old, announced, "I'm going to marry Patrick when I grow up."

Minty's mother and Patrick's father had laughed. But Patrick—six years older—had said, "I'll wait . . ."

Minty knelt on the cushion before the altar and discovered that she was still holding her mug of coffee and half a piece of bread. Oh dear! She hadn't meant any lack of reverence. She thought God might even be amused that she'd brought bread and a drink when she came to His place on her first morning as owner of the Hall.

She gave thanks. For everything she'd received. For friends, especially for Patrick, who was the best friend she could ever have. She thanked God for the understanding, the forgiveness and the love that had finally come about between her father and herself.

She asked for protection from Simon. She tried not to think about what he might have done if Serafina hadn't been there.

She prayed for guidance. Patrick had been a wise counsellor since her return to the village, but last night he refused to advise her any more, saying she was a lot stronger and wiser than she thought. Surely he was mistaken? She was only a green girl. He was older than she and surely it wasn't wrong to rely on him when he knew so much more about, well . . . everything . . . than she did?

The only advice he'd given her—and she ground her teeth remembering what the infuriating man had said—was "Have a look at the books." What on earth had he meant by that?

The morning sun was warm about her. She relaxed. *Dear Lord, give me wisdom and understanding. You know the problems I have to face, the difficulties in the family . . . my stepmother Lisa . . . Simon's greed and ambition. My poor half-sister drifting through life. Everything about the house and estate is run down, everyone is looking to me for work and money . . .*

She remembered that Solomon had asked for wisdom when he succeeded his father David and felt comforted. Perhaps God would grant her a little wisdom, too.

She left the chapel cautiously, but there was no sign of Simon. For years he'd milked the estate to support his extravagant lifestyle, and when that crock of gold began to fail, he'd planned to lease the Hall to an American consortium to be run as a health farm, with himself as director of the company that was to run it.

Minty had to admit that she was afraid of Simon, not only because he thought she could still be his for the asking, but also because he was desperate for money and didn't care how he got it.

She pushed thoughts of Simon out of her head.

This was her first morning as Lady of the Hall, and she was going to make the most of it. Running down the stairs to the first floor, Minty opened the door into the room in which she'd been born. The four-poster bed stood against the inner wall, as it always had done. As a child she'd played on and in it with her mother. Even, sometimes, with her busy father.

The "bouncy" bed, they'd called it. This was not the great State Bed which the tourists would come to marvel at, but a lighter Victorian reproduction. The heavy cream curtains were not those embroidered by Eden women generations ago with green and blue flowers and fantastical birds on the important Jacobean bed, but were patterned in a William Morris design of willow leaves. When the curtains were let down, the bed made a private "house" in which to play.

Minty released the blinds at the windows which kept the room in shadow, and put her coffee mug down on the window-sill before unhooking the red rope which kept visitors away from the furniture. She smoothed the whitework counterpane only to discover it had been covered with a sheet of plastic.

She pulled the plastic off and climbed onto the bed to see if it still bounced. It didn't. It was unyielding and quite horrible. Yuk. She supposed it was historically correct to have a flock mattress on the bed, but it wouldn't be possible to sleep on it.

She wondered if Patrick would be amused by the idea of sleeping in the four poster—if she had a good mattress put on it—or if he would think it old-fashioned and inconvenient?

Patrick owned a red-brick, Virginia-creepered Georgian house in the village High Street nearby. His office and reception rooms were on the ground floor with his living quarters above. His furniture was antique but intended for daily use. You could flop into deeply cushioned chairs and put a mug of coffee on the floor without feeling like an intruder. Unlike life in her father's suite.

Minty had imagined she'd move into Patrick's home once they were married. Now she'd inherited the Hall, she didn't know what they'd do.

She looked at her watch. Half past eight. Was it still too early to ring him? She unhooked her mobile from her belt and at that moment he rang her.

"Minty . . . ?" No endearments, no enquiries after her well-being. "Have you any idea why the awe-inspiring Annie Phillips wants to see me this morning?" There was a clatter of cups in the background. "Your father's driver's just brought me a note, asking if I could spare her a few minutes at ten this morning. I'm quaking at the prospect."

He didn't sound as if he were quaking, but Patrick would crack a joke if he were facing a firing squad.

Minty pushed back her hair with one hand. "I've no idea. She asked me to meet her at eleven but she didn't say anything about seeing you. Can you fit her in?"

"With a bit of juggling. I've got an early bird in the office with me now—just making her a coffee. I'll ring when I'm finished, right?"

"Yes, but Patrick . . . what did you mean about looking at the books?"

He laughed and disconnected. Infuriating man!

Minty glanced at her watch and hurriedly inspected the other rooms on that floor. Each was beautifully presented, but somehow lifeless. There was no trace of the Eden family, whose home it had been for centuries.

The last room had been her grandfather's study. She remembered that in her childhood it had retained the scent of his tobacco though he'd been dead for some years. She'd often played hide-and-seek there, crawling into the cubbyhole of his great desk. His study was now just another bedroom, and she couldn't spot his desk at all. Perhaps it had been put into storage? She knew there was a great jumble of family bits and pieces in the east wing.

She couldn't see Patrick living in these rooms. Or herself, for that matter.

She retraced her steps and took the stairs down to the ground floor and the Long Gallery. This was where she'd danced with Patrick in a charity shop dress at the Ball. She lifted her arms and waltzed around, imagining herself still in his arms. She sang, "I could have danced all night . . ." Then laughed at herself.

In childhood this was where she'd run and played on rainy days. Could she still hear the echo of childish voices? Patrick had played with her, of course. Simon and his side-kick Miles had been the same age as Patrick, but they'd scorned to play with a little girl. There'd been other children? From the Manor?

Had they had a badminton net set up here? Had it been Patrick who'd taught her how to keep her eye on the racquet, never to take your eye off the shuttlecock? She grimaced. Hadn't Simon broken her racquet and lied that she'd done it herself? He'd been a nasty small boy even then, though so handsome that grown-ups never suspected what he was really like.

The sun had gone in and the oak floorboards looked dusty and neglected. She pulled up some of the window blinds and went to renew her friendship with the family portraits grouped over and around the two carved marble fireplaces.

Sir Ralph Eden had always been her favourite, swaggering away in his slashed doublet, the velvet cap on his head adorned with a fine red ostrich plume. Opposite him was the fair-haired heiress he'd married, in her stiff ruff and hooped skirt. Above the fireplace was her great-grandfather Edward Eden, who looked bad-tempered but apparently had been the gentlest of men. He'd been an Ambassador and died of typhoid in Constantinople.

She traced the family portraits down through the ages, as Eden followed Eden until at last the male line died out with her grandfather Ralph, who'd left the Hall to his only daughter, that pale butterfly Millicent Eden . . . who in turn had brought the wealthy financier Sir Micah Cardale into the family.

Millicent's portrait was not here. It had probably been banished to an attic, just as Minty had been banished to live with her uncle and aunt in the city. Sir Micah's portrait hung in the library opposite that of his second wife Lisa, but everyone else was here, including some relatives she didn't remember at all. But then, she'd only been five when she left.

The Edens were all fair of hair and blue of eye, with a strong chin— like Minty. None of them were spectacularly handsome or especially beautiful, but neither did they simper as sitters often did.

"You're terribly alike," said a voice behind Minty.

Minty whirled around. The girl behind her also jumped, blushing from high forehead to plump neck. She was more than a trifle overweight, had wispy fair hair inadequately held back with an elastic band and was dressed in a droopy black jumper and skirt. Her feet were encased in blue slip-ons and she was clutching a clipboard to her chest, which could have done with a better bra.

Minty held out her hand. "We met last night when I was introduced to everyone. You're in the Estate Office and your name is . . ."

"Tessa. Ms Phillips said you might need a personal assistant to help you with correspondence and would I report to you." She darted her eyes around. "You couldn't know, of course, but Mrs Kitchen—that's the housekeeper—will be furious that you've opened the blinds and let the light in. The cleaners are waiting to come in to make the place ready for opening time and Lady Cardale wants to see you, and Simon and your sister Gemma and oh, lots of people. And your father's housekeeper says you were expected for breakfast half an hour ago."

Minty knew which of those summons was important. She also decided that although she might need someone to help her, Tessa hardly looked bright enough for the job.

"I didn't realise it was so late." For a moment Minty was disorientated. "Which is the quickest way up to my father's rooms?"

Tessa led the way to the tower at the far end of the Gallery, where a modern lift had been installed beside the stairs for the benefit of disabled tourists. She pressed the button to summon the lift, her eyes twitching to Minty and away. "Everybody's afraid you're going to make a lot of changes, but you'll be guided by Simon, won't you? After all, he's been running the place for ever, and knows what's best."

So this was someone else who thought Simon was perfect. "Surely you don't want the Hall turned into a health farm?"

Tessa was beginning to relax. "The Hall is losing money, so why not? Someone said you were marrying Patrick Sands, but of course I didn't believe that."

"Why not?" The lift arrived, and they stepped inside.

"He's not at all good-looking or even rich, so you can't be serious about him."

Minty was amused. No, Patrick wasn't particularly good-looking, though she never thought of him in those terms. If you compared him to Simon, then Simon won in the looks department, but lost in any other.

"Patrick's my kind of man," said Minty, reducing Tessa to silence. "Well, Tessa, I've got a lot to learn and I'm sure you can be a great help. I need an office, a large diary, a telephone, a computer with access to the Internet. I need to make a list of all the people I ought to speak to ..."

"Oh dear, I don't know if ... I mean, I'm not sure how to ..."

Minty gritted her teeth. Her first impulse was to blast this incompetent girl to smithereens but pity stayed her hand. Tessa couldn't help it. "I'm sorry, I shouldn't have asked you. May I borrow your clipboard with the list of everyone who wants to speak to me? Thanks."

They reached the top landing. "Simon's rooms," said Tessa, pointing to the oldest, Jacobean wing. "The Estate Office is on the ground floor and if you don't need me, I'd better get back or someone will get into a terrible state."

She pointed to a door on the opposite side of the tower. "That's the east wing, with the Long Gallery on the ground floor and your sister Gemma's rooms above it. There's nothing on this top floor except junk but if you follow the corridor, it'll lead you back to the chapel and from there you can get into your father's rooms."

Minty raced along the dusty corridor, glancing at the collection of Victorian silhouettes of past Edens that hung between the windows. Some hung askew and one had fallen to the floor. She picked it up to replace it on the wall but found the wire was broken. She propped portly Sir Piers against the wall and glanced down into the Fountain Court below. She thought it was typical of Simon's reign that the superb fountain, brought back from Rome by one of her forebears, no long worked.

Crossing the landing by the chapel, she slipped back into her father's rooms. Serafina was waiting for her in her daytime black, hair neatly pinned into a chignon, fingers tapping on crossed arms. The glass-topped dining table was elaborately laid for one person.

Minty's first reaction was to apologise for being late, like a naughty child. Then she straightened her back. Serafina, Annie Phillips and Minty had sat through long hours together, nursing Sir Micah when he was dying. Minty respected Serafina but didn't fear her. Come to think of it, she was actually very fond of her.

So instead of an apology, she gave Serafina a hug. "I forgot the time, and now I'm ravenous. How long have I got before Annie wants to see me?"

"Long enough to eat." Serafina poured orange juice and opened a hostess trolley to display a full English breakfast.

Minty gulped juice, talking through it. "That girl Tessa. Apparently Annie thought she could be my personal assistant, but . . ."

"You won't want that one. Simon only took her on to please her grandmother who's got money, and Tessa adores him. Mrs Kitchen does, too. She's the housekeeper. Says she's 'going to put you in your place'. Best get rid of both while you can."

Minty dived into scrambled eggs and bacon. "I must give them a chance. I do need somewhere to work, though. I need to make phone calls. I want to get hold of the brochures for the Hall, and oh, a dozen things."

"Micah's sick room used to be his office. I've had it put back for you."

Minty grabbed toast with one hand and a coffee with the other. "Serafina, I love you!" She kissed the older woman's cheek. "Oh, before I go ... do you know why Annie Phillips went to see Patrick this morning?"

"She didn't say. I'll bring you some more coffee in a little while."

SINS *of the* FATHERS

JAMES SCOTT
BELL

ZONDERVAN   BESTSELLING AUTHOR OF **BREACH OF PROMISE**

James Scott Bell

James Scott Bell studied philosophy, creative writing, and film in college, acted in Off Broadway theater in New York, and received his law degree, with honors, from the University of Southern California. A former trial lawyer, Bell is the author of the Christy Award-winning *Deadlock*, a thriller about the Supreme Court, and the coauthor of the bestselling Shannon Saga series. He lives in Southern California with his wife, Cindy, and their two children.

A Word From the Author

An unspeakable crime by a thirteen-year-old boy . . .
A lawyer with a dark past assigned to defend him . . .
And a victim's mother whose faith is shattered . . .
Where is God in all of this?
That's the main question in *Sins of the Fathers.*

A struggling lawyer named Lindy Field begins to defend the thirteen-year-old boy. Is he a monster? Insane? Or is there something else going on beneath the surface?

As Lindy struggles with her spiritual and professional life, she gets closer to the troubling truth. And in the process becomes a target herself.

At the same time, I wanted to explore what goes on in the heart and mind of the mother of one of the victims. Mona Romney is a Christian, but her loss throws her down hard. Can her faith possibly save her . . . and her marriage?

Sins of the Fathers faces some of the hardest questions of life—why does God allow evil? How can I forgive the seemingly unforgivable? Can God truly heal the wounds of the past?

Set in the harsh world of the Los Angeles criminal courts system, *Sins of the Fathers* delivers conflicts and twists, and ultimately the truth about God's incredible mercy.

James Scott Bell

Chapter 1

1.

Lindy Field gunned her Harley Fat Boy, snaking through the congested Los Angeles traffic in the Cahuenga Pass. She'd bought the bike for days like this, when she was late getting downtown and the LA freeway system was pulling its asphalt-glacier routine.

Well, for that and because she just didn't see herself as a car person. Inside all the best defense lawyers, Lindy believed, was a hog engine revved to the limit. She could not abide the lawyers who putt-putted around the criminal courts, doing deals when they should have been chewing prosecutors' rear ends.

The way she used to. Maybe the way she would again, if the chips fell right for a change.

She made it to the Foltz Criminal Courts Building five minutes after her planned time of arrival and took off her helmet. She could feel her tight curls expanding. Security gave her red leather jacket with the Aerosmith patch on the back a skeptical once-over. They probably thought she was just another family member of some loser defendant here in the city's main criminal court center.

Of course, Judge Roger Greene's clerk, Anna Alvarez, knew her. She'd called Lindy to set up the meeting, the nature of which was still a mystery to Lindy. Anna stood at her desk in the empty courtroom and greeted Lindy like an old friend.

"Hey, there she is. Been too long."

"What is this place?" Lindy looked at the walls. "It seems somehow familiar."

"Yes, it's a courtroom. A place where strange lawyer creatures can sometimes be seen."

Lindy hugged Anna. "If a strange lawyer is what you want, I'm your girl."

"Good to have you back."

Was she back yet? *You need a case and client for that, don't you?* Lindy breathed in the familiar smell of carpet and wood and leather. Yes, familiar, yet oddly out of reach.

Anna took Lindy back to Greene's chambers. Greene embraced her like a father welcoming his child home as Anna returned to her desk.

Judge Roger Stanton Greene was fifty-seven, lean, with a full head of black hair streaked with imperial gray. Very judicial. Greene served in Vietnam as a Green Beret. Came back, finished first in his class at Stanford Law.

And he was one of the better judges in town. Actually fair toward people accused of crimes. That he continued to be reelected in law-and-order Los Angeles was something of a miracle. Lindy had tried a few cases before him as a PD, and he always seemed to be looking for ways to cut her a break.

"You look wonderful," Judge Greene said.

Lindy tossed her helmet on a chair. "You're a great liar, Judge. Ever think of going back into practice?"

He laughed and motioned for her to sit. His chamber was filled with books—not just law, but all sorts of subjects. Greene was one of the most learned men she knew.

"So how long's it been since you've tried a case down here?" Greene asked.

"A year. A little more."

"Get some skiing in during the off time?"

"I don't ski when I'm on meds. I tend to run into trees."

"Was it rough?"

Lindy inhaled deeply. She knew he was referring to her crash-and-burn after the Marcel Lee verdict, when she went from rising deputy public defender to thirty-two-year-old washout. "Yeah, it's been rough. But I beat it back with ice cream and Kate Hepburn movies. You'd be surprised what a little *African Queen* can do for the spirit."

"Who's handling the Lee appeal now?"

"Appellate Division. Menaster."

"He's good. If there's a way to get the thing reversed, he'll find it." Greene did not say it with much conviction. That was understandable. The days of frequent reversals were over. The fair citizens of California, demanding easy answers to a complex crime problem, were initiative happy. They passed laws that promised instant, get-tough results. They elected politicians and judges who strove to come down harder on crime than Torquemada. They passed bond measures to build more prisons to warehouse an ever-swelling population of hard timers and three-strikes losers.

And if a kid like Marcel Lee got tossed into that fetid swamp, so what? One more they wouldn't have to worry about being out on the streets.

Lindy felt that sensation that took over her skin whenever she thought of Marcel. *Fever skin*, her mother used to call it, when every pore felt sensitive and exposed. She couldn't will it away, so she settled into a chair like a swami lowering himself onto a bed of nails.

Greene sat behind his desk. "You have an office?"

"I pay a guy for a mailing address in the Valley, and use of his library and conference room."

"Hard to get started again?"

"Only thing I know for sure, making it on your own as a lawyer is not about competence."

"What's it about?"

"Overhead."

Greene nodded. "And getting clients."

"Oh yeah. I've heard of those."

"Why don't you do one of those lawyer commercials? Like that guy who used to have his clients say, 'He got me twenty million dollars.'"

"Right. I can see it now. One of my guys pops onto the screen. 'Lindy Field got me twenty years.'" It felt good to be talking plainly again.

Greene swiveled in his chair, smiled. "So you want to know why I wanted to see you?"

"Comic relief?"

"An assignment."

"Cool. *Court-appointed* means county pays."

"It's a juvenile matter."

An involuntary groan escaped Lindy's throat. "Judge—"

"Just hear me out."

"I don't want to do juvenile again."

"I understand. But there's something about this one. Does the name Darren DiCinni mean anything to you?"

Lindy's jaw dropped like a law book falling from a shelf.

"That's right," Greene said. "The one who killed those kids at the baseball game."

Lindy tried to wipe the shock off her face. Was he actually asking her to rep the thirteen-year-old whose face was all over the news?

"Won't the public defender handle it?"

"There's a conflict."

"How?"

"The boy's father, Drake DiCinni, was repped by the PD's office for something that got dismissed a year ago. So they can't do it. Even if they could, I'd want you."

Lindy closed her eyes for a moment, trying to keep the office from closing in around her head. "But there are so many others you could tap."

"I know this is not your average juvi case. But you have a way with them."

"Had."

"You still do. You don't lose that touch, Lindy, no matter what. And this kid's going to need special handling."

"He said God told him to kill the people?" That's what she'd read in the *Times*.

"Right."

"He connected to some cult or anything?"

Greene shrugged. "I only know what's been reported."

Lindy paused, then shook her head slowly. "I just don't think I'm ready for something this heavy."

"There's one more thing. The deputy handling this is Leon Colby."

The name hit her like a spear. It took a long moment for Lindy to remove it. And then she felt the old wound, the one shaped like Marcel Lee. Colby prosecuted the Lee case, sent the boy away for life.

"This is some kind of weird *Twilight Zone*, right?" Lindy put the heel of her palm on her forehead. "I'm going to be getting out of this universe soon, right?"

"I know what you must be thinking."

"Really? You know? From on high?"

Greene said nothing.

"I'm sorry," Lindy said. "That was a rotten thing to say."

"It's okay. I completely understand. Why don't we just forget it?"

Yes, forget it. Leave now before you change your mind. Leon Colby? Why had Greene even considered asking her?

Maybe because he knew the thought of Colby coldly scavenging the bones of another kid almost made her gag.

"Hey," Greene said, "there's a great play at the Taper. Have you seen—"

"I'll see him," Lindy said. "Once. And I'm not promising anything."

"Lindy, you don't have to—"

"Don't press your luck, Judge. Where is he now?"

2.

The last time Lindy was in Men's Central Jail was during the Lee case, right after Marcel attempted suicide.

Why wouldn't he? This was no place for juveniles. That was the whole reason for having Juvenile Hall. But when the kids were tried as adults, Los Angeles threw them in Men's Central, downtown, where they spent twenty-three-and-a-half hours a day locked in windowless four-by-eight-foot cells.

Death-row inmates at Quentin had it better. Career criminals at Pelican Bay were on easy street by comparison. All those guys got ample time each day for showers, phone calls, and a walk in the corridor in front of their cells. Not the juvis in Men's Central.

Lindy remembered when the *Times* did a story on the horrible conditions behind the steel door of Module 4600 at Central, which guarded the two tiers of twenty-four cells where the juvis were housed. Four, five, or six to a cell. Some of the local politicians jumped on it and beat their chests for change. It gave them a couple days' publicity.

And change did happen. For a time. Most kid-adults were taken to Sylmar, a juvi lockup, and that seemed to make everybody feel good. But pretty soon the bottom line snapped its jaws tight around the situation: It cost more to put kids out there.

So little by little, the warehousing of juvis in Men's Central—isolated from the adult population, of course, but crammed inside those cells that had only a toilet, a thin foam mattress, and what the County had the temerity to call bedding—little by little, the dumping of kids no one had any sympathy for returned. And without the *Times* making hay, the politicians kept quiet.

There was no rousing plea to be kinder to juvenile criminals.

He didn't look like Lindy had pictured. When he was marched into the interview room, shackled and in his orange jailhouse jumpsuit, he was a lot smaller than she thought he'd be. Lindy estimated he was about her height. Which wasn't good for him. If he got sent to prison—and Lindy knew that was the most likely outcome, even if Clarence Darrow came back from the dead to defend him—Darren DiCinni was not going to last long. He'd be fresh meat, tossed into a pit of ravenous lowlifes with nothing left to lose.

"Twenty minutes," the deputy sheriff said as he put Darren's hands in the desk cuffs. The jail classified juveniles as K–10s, highest security, and kept them isolated. The deputies claimed it was because juvis did the crazy things, to prove themselves to the older inmates. Darren was also a "high power" inmate, one with notoriety and media coverage. He needed to be protected from prisoners who might want to make a name for themselves by taking out a celebrity killer.

She tried to read his face. Who was Darren DiCinni, beside some teenager lost in oversized coveralls? Who was this boy sitting on the steel stool on the other side of the wire-mesh Plexiglas in the green interview booth, accused of an abominable crime? How did he get to this place?

She always asked herself these questions about new juvenile clients. They were only a step or two removed from childhood, yet they did evil things.

Why?

He did not look at her.

Lindy leaned toward the talk holes in the Plexiglas. "Darren, I'm Lindy Field. I'm your attorney."

His eyes did not move. He was staring at the floor like some sort of comic-book character who could cut through stone with laser beams shot from his eyeballs. Lindy suddenly had no trouble believing he had killed six people in cold blood.

"I'm here to talk to you about your case."

No change.

Lindy had handled bad ones before, ones with attitude, with chips on shoulders the size of buses. But she'd always managed to penetrate the barriers, at least a little bit, to a level where she could communicate.

Some were tougher to get to than others, that was all.

Darren DiCinni was going to be one of the tougher ones.

"Look, you don't have to talk to me now, but at some point we're going to have to get together on this thing. The DA isn't going to look out for you. The cops aren't. Your lawyer is, but you've got to give me something. Remember, anything you say will stay with me. I won't talk about it with anybody else."

That was always the first move. Establish trust. Cast yourself on their side.

DiCinni didn't move.

There was something strange here.

Despite his inner fires, Darren DiCinni didn't have a bad-boy aura. His light brown hair was trimmed and neat. He was a skinny kid too, stuck in that awkward stage between child and young man. His hands and wrists looked like they could slip right out of the shackles, like toothpicks from a wedding band. And his face, cool and impassive, was almost translucent, like baby skin.

Darren DiCinni was not, at first glance, like the tattooed and scarred outlaws she was used to. Nor was he trying to be.

But the peculiar thing was, he wasn't some tragic innocent, either. A few years ago, another young, skinny kid had shot up a school down near San Diego. He looked so young, so impossibly young to do such a thing.

DiCinni might have seemed that way too, except for those eyes. And that made him impossible to for Lindy to peg.

There was a reason he did not fit into any apparent slot, and Lindy had to find out what that was. She had the feeling the answer would be her—and DiCinni's—only hope of getting a more favorable sentence than life in prison.

"Darren, I'm going to talk to the DA about your case. I need to get to know you just a little. I want you to know you can trust me."

Nothing. Those lasers bored into the floor.

Maybe there was a competency issue here. Maybe DiCinni wouldn't have the capacity to help with the defense, and she could get him into a mental facility, keep him out of prison.

"You gonna talk to me today, Darren?"

She waited. And then, slowly, DiCinni shook his head. He still had not looked at her.

Lindy wanted to reach through the glass and grab him, shake him. She wanted to rouse him out of his stupor, force him to pay attention, make him realize he was dangling over a gorge by a string. And, she realized, to make him help *her*. She didn't want to lose another one like she lost Marcel Lee.

"Please, Darren. Let me help you. That's what I'm here for, that's what I do. I went to law school and everything. I had seven years with the public defender's office. Will you just give me something to work with here?"

DiCinni looked up. She now could see his eyes were brown speckled with flecks of green. They were still shooting hot beams, but with something added. A probing.

She let him look.

Then Darren DiCinni started rattling his desk cuffs. Violently.

"Darren—"

The metallic clatter got louder.

"Stop, Darren."

He did not stop.

The deputy charged over and slapped Darren's back. "Cut it out."

"I wanna go back," Darren said. His voice was high, like a choirboy's.

"Darren, you have to talk to me sometime."

He glared at her with a mix of defiance and confusion. The deputy began to undo the shackles.

"Darren, wait."

The deputy looked at Lindy with disdain. "Says he's through, he's through."

Lindy put her hand on the Plexiglas. "Wait a second."

But the deputy already had the desk cuffs off. Darren got up quickly and didn't look back as he was led away.

Outside Men's Central, the harsh glare of the LA afternoon sun hit her eyes like a police interrogation light. The kind cops used to coerce confessions in those old B movies. *Why don't you just admit it, Lindy? Come on, you know it, we all know it. You lost your chops when they put you in the psych ward. You don't have what it takes. Your father knew it all along, didn't he? Tried to tell you. What've you got to prove, Lindy? Give it up. You can't help anybody, especially this kid who rattles chains at you.*

She had to get to her bike. The growl of her Harley was the only thing that could drown out her thoughts this day. But she knew, with a harsh, prophetic certainty, that no sound was going to help her this time.

DON BROWN

TREASON

IN THE COURT-MARTIAL OF THE CENTURY, JAG OFFICER
ZACH BREWER FACES AMERICA'S TOUGHEST ENEMY YET.

ZONDERVAN

Don Brown

Don Brown spent five years in the U.S. Navy as an officer in the Judge Advocate General's (JAG) Corps. During that time, he served with the U.S. Attorney, served in the Pentagon, and was published in the Naval Law Review. Each is an opportunity few JAG Corps officers ever experience; combined, they have given Brown an exceptional vantage point not only of the Navy, but also of the inner workings of powerful "inside-the-beltway" political operations in Washington. Leaving active duty in 1992 to pursue private practice, Brown remained on inactive status through 1999, rising to the rank of Lieutenant Commander. Currently he and his family live in North Carolina, where Brown operates his own law firm, Brown & Associates, PLLC, and explores his newest endeavor: writing novels.

A Word From the Author

JAG officer Zack Brewer is as tough as they come-but is he tough enough to take down terrorism? He's about to find out ...

When radical Islamic clerics infiltrate the Navy Chaplain Corps, inciting active duty soldiers to acts of terrorism, the Navy ends up on the line. With so much at stake, the Navy JAG knows there's only one choice for prosecutor: Lieutenant Zack Brewer. His assignment? Prosecute the infiltrators to the fullest extent of the law for treason and murder.

Much to Zack's chagrin, his staunchest rival, Diane Colcernian, is appointed his assistant prosecutor. The tension between them mounts as they take on internationally acclaimed civil defense lawyer Wells Levinson. But when Zack and Diane finally agree to put aside their animosity, they end up in even more trouble than ever.

Caught in emotionally charged circumstances, aware his every move is being watched and analyzed, Zack soon realizes this case will challenge the very core of his skills-and of his Christian beliefs. Beliefs that could cost him everything.

The stakes are high ... and the entire world is waiting for the verdict.

Don Brown

Chapter 1

Lieutenant Zack Brewer, JAGC, USNR, checked his watch.

The slow-crawling traffic on Harbor Drive, a six-mile route along San Diego Bay connecting the 32nd Street Naval Station to "COM-NAVBASE" headquarters downtown, was not cooperating with Vice Admiral John F. Ayers's penchant for punctuality.

Brewer checked his watch again. *Twelve minutes.*

When the brake lights on an old rusty Toyota flashed red just inches in front of his Mercedes, Brewer's foot hit the antilock brakes. The sudden jolt thrust him forward, tightening the shoulder harness across his chest, which tempted him to utter a phrase not customarily used in most Sunday school classes. He refrained.

He hit his horn. The shrill blare prompted the Toyota driver, in denim work clothes, to turn around and glare through the window. Zack chuckled and managed a grin as he gave the man a half-wave of apology.

A few minutes later, he wheeled his Mercedes into the parking lot at the corner of Broadway and Harbor Drive. Brewer snatched his leather briefcase off the backseat, slammed the car door, and briskly walked toward the entrance of the building.

Two shore patrol sailors, each flanking the front door of the building and dressed in crisply starched white uniforms with pixie cup hats, came to attention, then flashed sharp salutes.

Zack shot back an equally sharp salute, then passed through the entrance of the building, under a large navy blue and white sign that read "COMNAVBASE SAN DIEGO."

The chief petty officer manning the security station in the main lobby rose to his feet. "May I help you, Lieutenant?"

"Lieutenant Brewer for a meeting with Admiral Ayers and Captain Morrison at ten hundred hours."

"Identification please, sir."

Brewer handed the chief his armed services identification card, then checked his watch as the chief picked up the telephone. "Lieutenant Brewer for Admiral Ayers."

The chief hung up and glanced at Zack. "They'll be ready in five minutes. You know the drill, Lieutenant. Sixth deck. First door on your right."

Brewer stepped in the elevator and punched the number. A moment later the aluminum doors parted, and he stepped out into a large, anti-septic-smelling hallway. He checked his watch again. Just enough time to stop by the head for a last-minute uniform check. The admiral was a stickler for detail—more than once, officers had been dismissed for the slightest infraction of dress.

He stepped to the mirror and turned for a closer inspection of his short-sleeved summer whites. The black shoulder boards bearing the two full gold stripes and the JAG insignia were in place.

His salad row, the row of ribbons displaying his individual medals and achievements, though not as full as that of a twenty-year sea dog, was impressive for a junior JAG officer. There was a pink and white Merito-rious Defense Service Medal, a green and white Navy Commendation Medal, a green and orange Navy Achievement Medal, a multicolored Sea Service Ribbon, and an orange and yellow National Defense Service Medal. The impressive array of colors was penned perfectly on two rows of bars on the breast of his white shirt just above the pocket.

He checked to see if the right side of his gold belt buckle was aligned with the gig line of his zipper and the line of buttons up the front of the white shirt.

He frowned at his shoes and snatched a paper towel from the dis-penser, doused it with water, added a couple of drops of soap, and with one swipe transformed the toe of his right shoe into the same ice-cream white color dominating the rest of his uniform.

Then he stepped back for a final assessment. The U.S. Navy's sum-mer white uniform, resplendent with black and gold shoulder boards, was the second-best-looking military uniform in the world. Only the Navy's formal "choker" white uniform—the one worn with ceremonial swords—looked better. He had one of those too, hanging in his closet at home.

Neither Tom Cruise nor Richard Gere had anything on Zack Brewer today. He mentally pronounced himself shipshape, then headed back to the hallway, turned right, and marched into the reception area of Admiral Ayers's office.

A moment later, a lieutenant in summer whites stepped out of the admiral's inner sanctum and into the reception area. The aide-de-camp's uniform was identical to Zack's except for the gold rope looping around his right shoulder, signifying he was an admiral's aide. "The admiral is ready for you now, Lieutenant."

Zack nodded to his brother-in-arms, then walked through the entrance to the admiral's richly paneled office, came to a halt under the gold chandelier about five feet in front of the officer's desk, and stood at attention. The admiral was sitting behind his large mahogany desk. In strict compliance with Navy protocol, Zack bored his eyes three feet over the admiral's head, finding a spot on the back wall. With his peripheral vision, he noticed two other Navy captains in khaki uniforms in the office. He recognized Captain Tom Morrison, who was standing by the window holding a steaming cup of coffee. The other, whom he did not recognize, bore the insignia of a Navy SEAL on his khaki uniform shirt and sat in a large leather chair just to the left of the admiral's desk.

"Lieutenant Brewer reporting as ordered, sir."

"At ease, Lieutenant," Ayers said. "You know my personal JAG officer, Captain Tom Morrison?"

"Yes, sir, quite well." Zack exchanged a pleasant nod with Morrison, who was sipping his coffee by the window.

"And I'd like you to meet Captain Buck Noble." The admiral gestured toward the captain seated in the leather chair. "Captain Noble is commanding officer of Navy Special Warfare School in Coronado."

"Lieutenant." Noble stood and extended his hand to Brewer.

Two seconds later, Zack almost grimaced as he withdrew his hand from Captain Noble's vicelike grip.

"Please sit. No need to be overly formal here, Counselor." The admiral waved Zack to a chair in front of his desk.

Ayers nodded to Captain Morrison. "Captain, care to brief the lieutenant on what we have here?"

"Certainly, Admiral." Morrison took a sip of coffee. "There's been a rape over at the amphibious base." He paused.

"Yes, sir?"

"We'd like you to prosecute."

It sounded routine. So why call him down here to meet with the admiral and Captain "Grip"?

"I've explained to the admiral and the captain that, in my opinion, you're the best man for this. You were awarded the Navy Commendation Medal for the great job you did in that *Jones-O'Leary* rape prosecution involving the dental technician down at the Naval Station."

"Just doing my job, sir."

"In this case, Lieutenant, your job is complicated by the victim."

"I don't follow you, Captain."

Captains Morrison and Noble exchanged glances as Admiral Ayers rocked back in his chair, folded his arms, and stared at Zack.

"Your victim, Lieutenant, is an officer," Admiral Ayers said. "An Annapolis graduate. Deputy Public Affairs officer for the Naval Air Station at North Island. The matter is complicated most by her uncle."

"Her uncle?"

"Ensign Marianne Landrieu's uncle is United States Senator Roberson Fowler."

Zack gulped, then inhaled slowly. "Democrat? Louisiana? Ranking Minority Member? Senate Armed Services Committee? Roberson Fowler?"

"One and the same." The admiral looked at Captain Noble. "Captain, you want to take it from here?"

Noble gave the admiral a brisk nod, then turned to Zack. "The animal that did this is one of ours. A Navy SEAL." His voice reflected his disgust. "We want this maggot nailed, Lieutenant. We want his heart cut out. His head served up on a platter. Understand?"

"Loud and clear, sir." If he didn't deliver, it would be *his* head on the platter in place of the maggot's. "With respect, Captain Noble, the Uniform Code of Military Justice allows imposition of the death penalty for a rape conviction."

"Really?" Noble's eyebrows rose.

"Yes, sir. Article one hundred twenty of the UCMJ technically provides for death or life imprisonment for a convicted rapist. The convening authority would have to request it, and we'd have to notify the defense in advance. I've been waiting for the right case to come along."

A slight smile crept onto the tough SEAL commander's battle-hardened lips. "I think we'll get along just fine, Lieutenant."

"Now hang on a minute." Captain Morrison leaned forward. "Lieutenant Brewer's aggressive reputation precedes him. He's right. The death penalty is technically an option for a rape conviction under military law. But then again, that's true for convictions for murder, mutiny, desertion, and treason. With respect, Admiral, you would be the first Navy convening authority to seek the death penalty for rape since World War II. It may look like political pandering to a powerful senator if we do. Besides, Roberson Fowler opposes capital punishment."

Admiral Ayers lifted his hand, calling for a moment of silence. "I agree with Captain Morrison. I'm not going to be the first Navy convening authority since the war to go capital on a rape charge. But it *is* good to see the Navy JAG Corps is well represented by both the aggressive young tiger *and* the seasoned gray owl."

When the obligatory chuckles subsided, Zack nodded. "May I ask about the status of the Article 32 Investigation, Admiral?"

"By all means, son. That's why you're here. I want our game plan in place before you head back down to Thirty-second Street," Ayers said, referring to the 32nd Street Naval Station, the largest of all the military installations around San Diego. He gestured to Morrison. "Why don't you take this one, Tom?"

"Yes, sir, Admiral." Morrison turned to Zack. "The Article 32 has been completed, Lieutenant. The investigating officer found probable cause to proceed with a charge of felony rape." He paused. "And I might add, he had his hands full with this investigation."

"Sir?"

"This could be messy, Lieutenant. The perpetrator, a Petty Officer Antonio Blount, is claiming consent."

Zack frowned. "An officer and an enlisted SEAL."

"It gets messier, Zack. This one is interracial."

"How so?"

"Caucasian victim, Filipino-American perpetrator."

"It's not as hard to believe as the officer-enlisted thing," Zack mused. "But an ensign fresh out of the Academy risking captain's mast by romantically fraternizing with an enlisted man? Unbelievable, even if the enlisted man is a SEAL."

"Good point, Lieutenant," Morrison said.

"But there is one positive thing about a consent defense, gentlemen." Zack had their attention. "If the accused claims consent as a defense, that means he must testify. If he testifies, I get to cross-examine him." He paused, looking directly at Captain Noble. "That, Skipper, is where I will cut his heart out for you. And with all due respect, sir, you'd better believe I will."

"Somehow," Ayers said, "I think he means it."

"I like your killer instinct, Brewer." A half grin eased across Noble's features. "Ever think about a cross-designation transfer into the SEALS?"

"The SEALS are the finest special warfare unit in the world, Captain."

"I hate to pour water on this mutual admiration society," Captain Morrison said, "but there's one other thing I think you need to know, Lieutenant. Defense counsel has been appointed." Captain Morrison pursed his lips. "Lieutenant Colcernian is representing the accused."

Zack's smile faded, and a grunt escaped his lips.

Captain Noble eyed him. "You have a problem with that, Lieutenant?"

"My apologies, sir. It's just that Lieutenant Diane Colcernian and I are—how should I say this diplomatically?"

"Out with it, son," Ayers ordered.

"Professional rivals." He weighed his words. "We go way back. We're in for a real war here, gentlemen."

"I hope you're still convinced we can win."

"Captain Noble, I've beaten Colcernian before. I know her game. We will win. It'll be a battle, sir, but at the end of the day, I'll give you your man with a big fat conviction stamped across his head. It doesn't really matter who the defense counsel is, sir."

"Well then," Admiral Ayers said, "on that note, it seems we've covered all relevant information for now, Lieutenant. Unless Captain Morrison has anything else?"

"No, sir." Morrison leaned back. "Lieutenant, I'll have the Blount file couriered to your office at Thirty-second Street this afternoon."

"Aye, sir."

"Very well then," the admiral said. "That will be all, Lieutenant."

So dismissed, Zack rose from his chair and stood at attention. "By your leave, sir."

"Permission granted, Lieutenant. You are dismissed."

As Zack turned and marched out of the admiral's office, his mind was consumed with the image of fiery, angry green eyes. Diane Colcernian was a beauty. One who'd accused him of stabbing her in the back when he'd beaten her in the final round of the Naval Justice School trial advocacy competition.

Her words still rang in his memory: *"I don't know when or how, Lieu-tenant, but I'll get you for this. And when I do, the stakes will be even higher. If I were you, I'd watch my back."*

That was two years ago. And though both were stationed in San Diego, and though he was the best prosecutor and she was the best defense counsel in San Diego, they had yet to go head-to-head in court.

Until now.

Now they'd face each other in a high-stakes court-martial that would be scrutinized by the Navy's top brass because of the victim's uncle.

The elevator opened on the first deck of COMNAVBASE head-quarters, and Zack stepped out, past the chief who was manning the reception desk and into the warm, arid Southern California sunshine.

Not that he was the least bit intimidated by Diane Colcernian, Zack thought as he returned the simultaneous salutes of the two shore patrol-men guarding the entrance of the building, but this trial was going to be a bloodbath.

A monumental bloodbath.

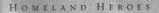

Two women. A friendship forged in war,

destroyed by a dark secret. Now one's fear of

God and the other's faith in Him collide in a

different kind of war— and only one of them can win.

WOUNDED HEALER

DONNA FLEISHER

ZONDERVAN

Donna Fleisher

As a veteran of the U.S. Air Force and the Air National Guard, Donna Fleisher loves crafting novels packed with excitement, strong and independent female characters, and the truth of God's persevering love and grace. Through her novels, Donna's goal is to help readers see that having the God of heaven romance us with his love is the most awesome joy one can fathom. Donna lives in Oregon.

A Word From the Author

Surrounded by the oppressive terrain, weather, and tension of Operations Desert Shield and Storm, soldiers Erin Grayson and Christina McIntyre shared a special bond. But when an ugly secret from Chris's past shattered their close friendship, they went their separate ways without even a good-bye.

Chris has spent her entire life running from the past, hiding her deepest secrets from those who care for her most. And now, five years after the war, tragedy has once again stolen her hope for a new life. She's ready to end it all.

It's a good day . . . to die.

Overcoming her own anger and doubt, Erin rushes to Chris's Colorado cabin. When Chris's fear of God and Erin's faith in him collide, they are involved in a different kind of war that only one of them can win. As Chris wrestles with grief, fear, and ghosts from the past, Erin fights to pull her from the brink of self-destruction. She will not lose Chris again.

Chris's life is at stake . . . as well as her soul.

For all who are hurting from past abuses, for all who are struggling to help a friend find Christ. For all the military veterans and their families, for all who are serving, for all who are waiting for a loved one to return, for those whose wait has ended in tragedy. God's love is for you. This story is for you.

May he hold and keep you.
Donna Fleisher

Chapter 1

*C*hristina McIntyre. Good. She still knew her own name.

Arms, legs, fingers and— She wiggled her toes. Good. Still intact.

She opened her eyes slowly, blinking, carefully, trying to focus.

The cabin. Timmons Trail. She knew where she was.

Why was she on the floor? She started to lift up but froze as a bolt of agony ripped through her front to back, top to bottom. Breath stuck in her throat as her eyes pinched shut; she fell back and for a full minute did not move.

This . . . is not a dream. I'm really hurt. How? What happened?

Cold darkness surrounded her. Night had fallen.

This . . . is not good. I am so late.

Her breath came in puffs. Sharp stabs knifed deep through her right side with each new breath, as fear trickled into her blood. Carefully, she brought her hands around to check the damage.

Her hands were bare. Where were her gloves? Her fingers ached with cold. It didn't make any sense. The long-sleeved thermal shirt she wore under her bright red San Juan Search and Rescue jacket usually kept her warm enough, even on the coldest nights.

Her jacket was gone.

Panic swelled inside her, stealing her breath, returning it only in short gasps. Pain split through her with every breath. She reached her left hand around to feel for damage. She winced. If ribs weren't broken inside her, they were cracked. She lifted her hand and felt the back of her head. The lump she found there triggered a rush of rote emergency procedure through her mind. *Blunt force trauma to the head—loss of consciousness, moderate duration—contusion, severe swelling, possible con—* She forced it all away, silently mumbling, *Yeah, yeah, yeah.* She lowered her hand. *I'll survive. Just . . . breathe.*

She needed her flashlight. In the deepening darkness, she could tell the door of the cabin was open wide. *Did I come through the door and fall?* One of the table chairs lay on its side by her feet. Did she knock it over as she fell? Fall on top of it? That could explain possible broken ribs. And then she hit her head on the floor and passed out? Had she always been this clumsy?

Closing her eyes, she could have slept, if it wasn't for the nagging stabs in her side.

She needed help. This irritated her. She hated even the thought of it—the rescuer needed rescuing. Because she tripped over her own big feet. The guys would love this. They'd want to haul her out on a litter just to embarrass her. She cringed.

But if someone didn't help her down off this mountain, she didn't think she would make it home.

That's just great. And we were supposed to go out tonight. Mexican with Travis. Her stomach churned and she groaned. That would be the last straw, throwing up all over the floor of the cabin.

Get up and get to the radio. Nothing to it. Every cabin in the San Juan District Three Search and Rescue region had a radio. If she could just stand up. Maybe she should light the kerosene lamp first. She needed to find her jacket.

If she could just stand up.

Grunting, panting, squeezing tears from her eyes, hoping no one was watching or listening to her pathetic display, she forced herself up and steadied herself against the table.

Light the lamp first, find my jacket and gloves, then call for help. Easy plan. As she made her way around the table to the other side of the cabin, the plan started to concern her. Maybe not so easy after all. The kerosene lamp hung from a hook that had been screwed into the ceiling. The cabin was small but, at five-foot-six, Chris would have to stand tiptoe to reach the lamp's metal hanger. As she reached her left hand up, her ribs twisted, and she almost fell to her knees. The pain seemed to swirl around her; her mind seemed to be shutting her body down without her consent.

She tried again. Reached the lamp and lowered it to the table. Now all she needed was a match. Her teeth ground as she carefully felt her way in the darkness to the supply cache along the cabin's back wall. She lugged open a heavy drawer and rummaged. Stumps of candles, string, a potato peeler, a deck of cards, a small plastic sewing kit. Matches had to be there. She had brought up a new pack of fifty boxes wrapped in a Ziploc only the week before last. She couldn't find them.

Cursing, she gave up. She could work the cabin's radio in her sleep. She inched her way to it, feeling for the box, but jerked her hand back when her finger sliced across something sharp. The sudden movement froze the breath in her lungs and, again, she waited, sucking at the blood that welled up from the cut.

Broken glass was not a good thing. A sick sense of dread flooded her stomach. The radio was old, vintage Vietnam era, but it worked fine. Encased in a box with a glass top and aligned only to be heard by San Juan District Three radios, it was available to anyone who needed it in an emergency. Carefully, Chris felt for the radio's microphone. She couldn't find it. The cord was there, and she followed it out until it abruptly ended. It had been cut.

The fear trickling through her gushed into a torrent.

Standing there, steadying herself against the table, gasping for air and wincing at the agony of it, sick to her stomach and weary beyond belief, she tried to focus on what had become her reality.

One more radio. And her flashlight. Out at the snowmobile. And, she hoped, her jacket. And her gloves. She headed outside, eased herself down the stairs and across the slippery snow-packed ground to her snow machine. She clicked on the snowmobile's headlights and winced at the sudden brightness. She reached for the radio microphone. Without tethered resistance, the mike felt weightless. Terror seized her. Her knees gave out, and she turned just in time to sit on the snowmobile's wide seat.

The radio mike cord had been cut. She dropped the useless mike into the snow, then reached back into the storage compartment. The flashlight, flares, and solar blanket—all gone. Even the small chain saw she carried to clear blowdown was gone. The snowmobile's keys were in her jacket pocket. Her jacket was no where to be found. She couldn't even find one glove.

She sat still, silent. Eyes wide. *Breathe. Focus. Think!*

Perfect silence filled the night, loud, ear-ringing silence. Faint swirls of fine, floating snowy powder caught her eye as a light breeze carried them across the headlight beams. Mesmerized, she watched. Her eyelids felt laden with sand. She desperately wanted to sleep.

So quiet. So peaceful. Pain and terror and numbing cold cancelled each other out as she simply sat there, watching the night. In the distance, an owl hooted. Her lips almost smiled.

The silence felt oppressive. Nothing moved. Only the breeze. Until she heard a pop. Very faint. The kind of pop a knuckle makes. Or an ankle bone. Her entire being froze, strained to hear more, to see through the shadows.

Someone was out there. Someone was watching her.

She listened, barely breathed. Reached up and clicked the snowmobile's headlights off. Darkness fell so quickly, so completely, it stunned her. *Just wait,* she told herself. *Don't panic.* There was just enough waning twilight left, if she could wait and let her eyes adjust, she would be able to see.

She saw something, to her left; she looked, just as that something exploded with light—the beam of a powerful flashlight pointed directly at her face. She turned away, eyes pinched shut.

"Not how I was hoping this night would go."

Did she hear the words? A man's voice. And what he said? She almost laughed, thinking, *You can say that again.* Her eyes opened slowly, but she could tell the beam was still pointed directly at her. "Do you mind?" came out before she realized it.

"Oh. Sorry." The beam of light fell to the snow between them.

Chris turned her head—a man stood about fifty feet away. In the faint light reflecting back over him, she saw the brilliant red of a San Juan Search and Rescue jacket. "Oh, well, sure. That explains it. Thanks a lot."

"What?" He sounded concerned.

"Fits you well. But I'd like it back."

"Oh." The flashlight beam shook as the man shuffled from foot to foot for a second. "Yeah. Well, I needed it more than you did. The stuff I was wearing got wet."

"Sorry to hear that."

The man was quiet.

Chris stared at his shadowy form. As the beam of light cut across her view, her headache spiked. She missed what the man said. "What?"

"Back to the cabin. I'll build a fire. We both need to get warm. Right?"

Well, one of us anyway. The man was wearing her gloves, too.

"Let's go. In the cabin."

Chris looked up but couldn't summon the strength to move.

"Now. Let's go. In the cabin." The flashlight's beam swung to point the way.

As Chris sat there, a strange warmth seeped into her bones with every pump of her heart—coursing pumps of pure, building rage. Just who did this lunatic think he was?

"I said *now*. Get up and get back into the cabin. I'm not kidding."

She glared. Not only was the man a vandal and a thief, he was rude as well.

He started toward her, switching the flashlight to his left hand as he walked and then pulling off the glove on his right hand with his teeth. Spitting the glove away, he reached into the pocket of Chris's jacket and pulled out something that glimmered in the light.

He stopped a few feet from her. Chris saw what he now held in his right hand.

"Get in the cabin *now*. I'm not going to tell you again."

A 9mm handgun. Police issue. Or military. She glanced up, into the man's eyes. What she saw shattered her rage, laid bare her underlying terror.

The man slowly raised the pistol and pointed it at Chris's head.

She pushed herself up and trudged back to the cabin.

His day off and he was back at the station. Travis Novak still smiled. In a few minutes, Chris would be off work and they would share a corner table at Buen Tiempo, munching on chips and salsa and sipping cold drinks. Chris always sipped a margarita. She didn't hassle Travis that he didn't drink. He would savor his perfectly sweetened, perfectly lemoned ice tea. And then the chimichangas would arrive. He could hardly wait.

"Come on, Chris, our chimichangas are a callin'!"

Samantha Jeffries yelled back. "Stop it, Travis, you're making me hungry!"

He laughed. "Is Chris in there?"

"Nope. Just me and Mandy."

"Have you seen her?" He resisted the juvenile urge to look for himself.

"Nope. Not since roll call."

"Okay. Thanks." He pulled the door closed and headed down the hall to the main office of the San Juan District Three Search and Rescue station. Once inside, he leaned against the chest-high counter and said a quick hello to Carla Crawley before going to the wall beside Carla's cubicle to reach for the crew locator clipboard.

"Hey, Travis," Carla said without getting up. "What are you doing here on your day off?"

"Have you seen Chris?" Travis looked over the list of names and times on the locator.

"Not since this morning. She's out checking Tri-Lake and Timmons."

He didn't like what he saw. "She hasn't come back yet?"

"What?" Carla stood up and reached over the counter for the clipboard.

Travis handed it to her. "She put her ETA as three. But it's almost five."

Carla keyed the mike. "San Juan Three calling twenty-twenty-four. Twenty-twenty-four, come in please." They waited. Listened. Travis tagged the clipboard back up on the wall and leaned against the counter. Still no response. "San Juan Three calling twenty-twenty-four. Please respond."

Nothing but silence.

A thread of fear began to lace itself around Travis's heart. "Try her again."

Carla keyed the mike and repeated the call. They waited. Nothing.

"This can't be right." Travis moved around behind the counter and pulled the mike out of Carla's hand. He reached over her to the radio, spun the squelch, then reset it to where he thought it should be and keyed the mike. "Chris? Chris? This is Travis." He ignored Carla's irritation. "Chris McIntyre, can you hear me? Come in. Please. Chris, please respond."

They waited. Travis reached over and cranked up the radio's volume.

Only light static hissed from the two speakers above them. Basic radio silence.

The walk up the stairs had been bad enough, but sitting in the freezing, hard chair was beyond bad. Careful not to bend forward or twist or even to try to move her right arm, Chris squirmed in the chair. Her rage had melted, taking its warmth with it. As helplessness overtook her, she started to shiver, feeling the cold like never before. Usually she liked cold weather; she felt at home in the mountains of snow and ice. Right now she felt like ice, and the uncontrollable shivering did little to help.

The man stood across the table from her, leaning back against the wall of the cabin. He just stood there, watching her. He had put the gun back into the pocket of Chris's jacket and used one of her matches to light the kerosene lamp but, after that, he just stood and watched her.

Irritation shot through Chris's belly. She looked up at him as words shivered out of her mouth. "Are y-you g-going t-to light the f-fire?"

The man pulled out a cigarette and lit it with another of Chris's matches. After drawing in a deep drag, he said, "Nah. I don't think so. You can if you want."

Chris let out an exasperated breath and looked away. Tucking both hands under her armpits, she rode the fine line between wanting to live and not really caring anymore one way or the other. She let the shivering control her as she lowered her head, closed her eyes. Shutting everything else out, she focused only on helping her body reach down somewhere to find warmth.

A picture popped into her mind. A memory. She almost laughed. There was a time, a few years back, when she lay on an army cot in a parking garage in the middle of the world's busiest desert in nothing but shorts and a sleeveless T-shirt, drenched in her own sweat, panting like an old hound dog. Erin, too, in the cot right next to her. It didn't matter that Erin was an officer; in Saudi, the miserable heat and humidity had everyone panting, officers and enlisted alike.

Lieutenant Erin Grayson.

That's just perfect. Think about her when I'm ready to die.

Chris heard movement. Raised her head and looked up.

The man had taken off her jacket and thrown it on the table. "There." He said nothing more.

Chris's jaw dropped. She couldn't think. But she wasted no more time. She reached a trembling left hand out, holding her breath as she did, and pulled the jacket back to her chest. Chris quickly tugged the zipper up to her chin—still shivering, but immensely relieved. She loved this jacket. She looked up at the man. "D-Don't sup-pose you left the g-gun in the p-pocket?"

The man laughed out loud. Reaching around to his back waistband, he pulled the pistol out, then tucked it back where it came from. He leaned against the wall and crossed his arms over his chest. The cigarette hung in his lips, a curl of smoke forcing him to squint one eye.

Chris gave him a sneer.

"Ya know, you weren't supposed to wake up until after I was gone."

She gave voice to her first thought. "You can g-go. I w-won't t-tell anyone."

"I thought I hit you hard enough. Then the way you went over that chair. I mean, ouch. You were down and out. And then, not even three hours later, you're up. Man." A breath of laughter. "I hit guys in the joint that hard, they sleep for a week."

Chris closed her eyes for a second. *Just my luck. I have a hard head.*

"It won't be much longer now."

"Yeah. It w-won't be long. Everyone w-where I w-work knows w-where I am. They'll be here any m-minute." She believed every word, but through her fear and trembling, did she sound convincing?

The man laughed as he lit another cigarette. "My friends will be here long before that."

His voice didn't tremble at all.

In five minutes Travis Novak was suited up and ready to leave. It was a mile to the Timmons Trailhead, another six to the old Forest Service cabin on Uncompahgre Mountain. Half an hour. By then, darkness would be thick. He had to move quickly.

He rechecked his gear, verified a full fuel tank, then climbed aboard the station's slick new Ski-Doo, smiling a bit as he fired it up, hearing the powerful engine roar. He idled the engine down to a hum as he put out a quick radio check. Carla promptly told him he had better turn around; Travis took that for a "loud and clear" and signed off. He pulled on his helmet and gave Mike a thumbs-up as he revved the engine again. Then he settled in and let the snow machine carry him out of the staging area. It was hard not to feel exhilarated by the power and speed. But it quickly soured into pure fear.

He whispered a silent prayer as the machine slipped him into the falling darkness.

Travis knew the way to Timmons Cabin. In his eight years with San Juan Mountain Search and Rescue, he had traveled this trail probably a thousand times.

The snowmobile climbed and skitted through the packed snow; he leaned and twisted the machine around every tree and rock, along every crevice. His moves were automatic. He wasn't concentrating on the trail.

Please, God. Something's wrong. I feel it. She's never late. She calls in if she is. She's always prepared. Extra fuel, flares— He looked up quickly. *Keep an eye out, Novak. Watch for flares. Watch for stray tracks off trail . . . watch . . . Oh, please, Lord, be with her.*

He needed to concentrate on the trail. He couldn't. His mind held her there. Her eyes, dark and mysterious. Her smile. Her laughter. She didn't laugh nearly enough. She had such a terrific laugh. Fun. Full of life.

And sometimes, when she allowed herself to really let go, when she'd turn to look at him, her eyes seemed to reflect the most brilliant rays of the sun. Not always. Only when she would let them.

He liked her the moment they met, was intrigued. A young U.S. Army medic, she had just spent ten months in Saudi Arabia, in Operation Desert Storm. He knew nothing about her, but was drawn to her. She pushed him away, pushed everyone away—had her own place in the world and wouldn't let anyone else in.

Until that one night, two summers ago. They had just hauled out a drunken fool. The man had compound fractures of both bones in his lower left leg. His six drunken friends stayed on the mountain to continue their party, offering no help at all. Because the district's helicopter was unavailable, Chris and Travis hauled the man all the way down as he tossed and jerked in the litter.

Afterward, as the rescue truck disappeared down the gravel road, Travis sat, in an exhausted stupor, and Chris flopped backward into a patch of soft clover. She closed her eyes and, after a minute, started to laugh.

It was the first time he ever heard her laugh. He laughed with her; he couldn't help it. "What's so funny?"

She didn't move to respond. Didn't even open her eyes. "Can you believe they stayed up there? They didn't even care enough about their friend to follow him down."

Travis shook his head. "Some friends."

"I don't think I can get up."

He looked at her. She was drenched with sweat. Her nose was dirty, and her sun-bleached brown hair stuck out all over the place through her French braid.

Travis stretched out beside her and they just stayed there. Talking. About nothing. About everything.

Later that night, showered and starving, they picked up sandwiches at the deli and drove out past Box Canyon to watch the sunset. Then they watched the stars. The night was fine.

Travis swallowed hard, forcing down the tightness in his throat. He was getting close, but the closer he got the more worried he became. He prayed for her. Now. Always. There was such pain in her eyes, something

160

hidden deep inside she would not reveal. A memory. Something. Too much kept hidden. It seemed to eat at her. Weary her. But there were rare times, precious times, when she would relax around him, would just enjoy the moment they shared. Travis savored those moments. Allowed himself to be drawn in.

Her heart was hidden, yet tender. Her eyes were fierce, yet imploring. Her kiss . . .

He had to get there.

He prayed. He was five minutes away.

In Chris's present state, there was not one thing she could think of to prevent the night from turning plain ugly.

The man was too strong, too smart, and too quick. Maybe, outside, if she tripped him, got him down, she could kick him and get away. *Yeah. One kick on ice and down you go.* That plan did not hold promise.

She only hoped his friends would arrive; they would kill her, go away, and no one else would have to get hurt.

So this is how it ends

She closed her eyes and gave in to her weariness.

Until she heard the distant hum of a snow machine. Her eyes popped open as panic flooded her heart.

The man heard it too. He killed the light in the lamp, grabbed the flashlight, and stood in the cabin's doorway.

Chris couldn't move. Everything inside her felt rushed—breath, thought, hope. She focused on what she heard, waited for her eyes to work in the heavy darkness.

One snowmobile. A big one. Powerful, well-tuned engine.

The man cussing, storming down the stairs—out the door, Chris saw his long shadow thrown by the snowmobile's headlight beams. She pushed herself up and stepped carefully to the door.

"Shut it down!" he screamed. "Shut it down right now!"

Who was here? Did the guy always yell at his friends like this?

"Shut it down! Or I swear I'll kill you, right here!"

The snowmobile fell silent.

Still the man yelled. "Get up. Get up! Now!"

No, not one of his friends. Good chance it was one of hers. Squinting into the snow machine's powerful beams of light, Chris struggled to see who it was. Then someone moved, backed away from the light, arms out to his side, a man . . . wearing a bright red jacket. His face—! Chris's heart gave out inside her, as if she'd been kicked in the stomach.

Travis!

More yelling. "Get back! Back up. Hands up where I can see them!"

Oh, God, Chris prayed. Only she didn't know how to pray. Travis had tried to teach her. She didn't want to learn. Until now. "Oh, God," a whisper now, as breath barely found its way inside her, as she stumbled down the cabin's icy steps. *Travis, what are you doing here?*

The man fussed with Travis's snowmobile. Smaller beams from his flashlight crisscrossed the trees to her left. She picked her way toward Travis, blinking. Was it Mike standing there? Or maybe Danny? Had to be. It was Travis's day off. Wasn't it?

She heard his voice. "Chris! Are you all right?"

"Shut up!" came from the man before Chris could respond. He cursed and reached down into his boot.

Chris watched for a second, confused, then looked away and moved closer to Travis, drawn by the brilliant red of his jacket, by the warmth of his love.

A flash caught her eye. To her left, light glinted brightly off something metallic, something the man now held in his hand.

A knife.

With one quick swipe, he cut the snowmobile's radio microphone cord.

Someone moved in behind her, wrapped arms around her, softly surrounded her. Travis. His touch melted Chris all the way down to nothingness. She leaned into his chest, barely able to stay on her feet.

"No!" The man walked toward them, flitting the knife left and right in front of their faces. "Get away from her. Now!"

Chris felt Travis move away. No words were spoken.

"Get back! Keep walking!"

She couldn't move. Travis backed away from her. She watched him go. Wanted to cry.

"You and me, tough guy." Travis's voice was soft, yet strained. "Let's settle this. Between us. Let her go."

The man seemed to consider the words, then turned and flashed the knife in Chris's face. "Get back to the cabin. Right now. Do *not* make me say it again."

"That's it. Go, Chris." Travis's soothing voice reached deep inside her. "Go on. The two of us are just gonna stay out here and have a little discussion."

She couldn't move.

The man reached behind his back, pulled the gun out of his waistband, and thumped the barrel against Chris's forehead. "Go!" The gun clicked as he chambered a round.

"Chris! Go! Get out of here!"

Tears welled in her eyes. *Oh, God . . . please*. Whatever happened this night, someone was going to get hurt. With one last look at Travis, she turned and forced herself toward the cabin. One step, then another. Two more steps. Her foot slipped a little. Always careful on ice. Now she didn't care. Two more steps. Another.

And down she went.

Her world disintegrated into an explosion of agony, brilliant white light, rushing-roaring in her ears, total breathlessness like she had never known before.

How long did she lay there? What brought her back?

Curses, yelling, sounds of a fight. *No . . . God, no.*

Somehow, she turned, rubbed her eyes, trying to clear her head. Travis and the man were fighting, throwing each other around in the snow, kicking, punching, growling . . .

Chris covered her face with her hands and crushed her eyes shut. Visions of swirling sand, the roar of a helicopter, yelling, screaming—her best friend hit, down, bleeding—*Erin down . . . bleeding!*

Cursing herself, cursing death and life, she stood, pushed herself as close to the men as she dared.

She had to do *something*.

The snow machine. Did Travis bring flares? She rushed to it. Set off all three. Did he bring a chain saw? No. Flashlight. She grabbed it. She stuffed the solar blanket into her jacket pocket. First aid kit, out where she could find it. Nothing else of use. She rushed to her snowmobile. Flicked on its headlights.

The two men still struggled.

Chris could bring on some serious hurt with the flashlight, if nothing else. She'd throw herself on the man, give Travis time to—

A sickening sound stopped her, turned her stomach so quickly she gagged.

Both men were still. Her captor struggled to his feet and stumbled back, swaying.

Travis was still down.

Chris fell to her knees in the snow.

The man doubled over and hung his head out over his knees, coughing, spitting, panting...

Travis didn't make a sound. His eyes hung wide open, frozen.

Chris covered her mouth. A deep, wrenching groan coursed through her as tears flooded her eyes. Crawling on hands and knees, staring at the man she loved, she reached him—and she knew. No pulse on his neck. Steam floating up from the life pouring out of his chest.

It was done.

Life was dead. Hope. She floated in anguish.

Her head fell until her forehead touched his. Desperate weeping overtook her. Mired in it, she couldn't move or think or breathe or see ...

Then barely, so very distant, she heard sounds.

No, God. Don't take me back.

Horrible sounds. Closer now. Louder.

God, please! Just take me now.

And louder. Only a few feet away, the man continued to cough and hack and spit.

She slowly raised her head as everything inside her started to turn. White hot rage, pure and overpowering, pushed everything else from her mind. She forced herself up, cursed away her tears, stood.

Yes. She would settle things first. Then come back and die with Travis.

No matter what, tonight it would end.

She focused on the man's face. Saw a hint of wariness in his glare. She stepped away from Travis. Flexed her empty hands. Glanced at the man's right hand. Saw the long knife he still held. Saw the red. Looked away. Just for a second.

They stared at each other, until the man's eyes flicked to Chris's left, searching.

The gun.

Chris spun around—found it first. She raised it, but had to use her left hand to keep it steady.　　　　She forced her teeth to unclench. Aimed the pistol at the man's chest. Spoke clearly. "I'm gonna kill you."

Something flickered in the man's eyes. "Not if I kill you first," he said through a faint grin. "Come on. You don't wanna die, do you?"

"Throw the knife away." Chris tried to hold the pistol steady.

"Give me the gun."

She growled. "I am not giving you this gun."

The man spit into the snow. "My friends will be here any minute."

"I set off three flares. How long do you think it will take before *my* friends get here? Throw the knife away, and get on your knees."

"Nope."

Her rage waned. Her strength. Pain seeped in, then bolted through her side as her arms started to shake. She glanced down at Travis. Her eyes pinched shut. She began to fall apart, piece by piece. Drew in a deep breath. "Throw it away and get down on your knees!" Screaming the words cost her too much. She started to cry.

"Ahh, lady." The man relaxed his stance. "You're strong; I'll give you that. Believe me. I never wanted any of this to happen."

"Shut up." Chris could only whimper the words. The gun shook so violently, she squeezed hard to keep from dropping it.

"Just give me the gun."

Don't be afraid . . . slipped into her thoughts. *Today's a good day . . . to die.*

She blinked away her tears and looked into the man's eyes just to be sure.

Yes. He would kill her, given any chance.

No one would blame her if she killed this man. Right now. Pulled the trigger. Justifiable.

No one would mourn for her if he . . .

The gun came down. She had no strength left to keep it up. No desire anywhere inside her to kill another man.

No desire to stop him . . . from killing her.

She slowly looked away, slowly started to turn away. The man leaped at her, knife in the air, pointed down at her throat.

Chris raised the gun into his chest. And fired.

One Tuesday Morning

Karen Kingsbury

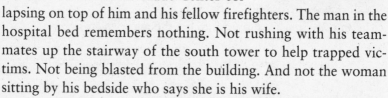

I'm a firefighter, God, so I know I've been in some tough places before. But this ... this not knowing the people I love ... this is the hardest thing I can imagine.

The last thing Jake Bryan knew was the roar of the World Trade Center collapsing on top of him and his fellow firefighters. The man in the hospital bed remembers nothing. Not rushing with his teammates up the stairway of the south tower to help trapped victims. Not being blasted from the building. And not the woman sitting by his bedside who says she is his wife.

Jamie Bryan will do anything to help her beloved husband regain his memory, and with it their storybook family life with their small daughter, Sierra. But that means helping Jake rediscover the one thing Jamie has never shared with him: his deep faith in God.

Jake's fondest prayer for his wife is about to have an impact beyond anything he could possibly have conceived. *One Tuesday Morning* is a love story like none you have ever read: tender, poignant, commemorating the tragedy and heroism of September 11 and portraying the far-reaching power of God's faithfulness and a good man's love.

Softcover: 0-310-24752-7

Unabridged Audio Pages® CD: 0-310-25402-7

Pick up a copy today at your favorite bookstore!

ZONDERVAN™

GRAND RAPIDS, MICHIGAN 49530 USA

WWW.ZONDERVAN.COM

A Riveting Story of Secret Sin and the Healing Power of Forgiveness

Oceans Apart

Karen Kingsbury

Airline pilot Connor Evans and his wife, Michele, seem to be the perfect couple living what looks like a perfect life. Then a plane goes down in the Pacific Ocean. One of the casualties is Kiahna Siefert, a flight attendant Connor knew well. Too well. Kiahna's will is very clear: before her seven-year-old son, Max, can be turned over to the state, his father must be contacted; the father he's never met, the father who doesn't know he exists: Connor Evans.

Now will the presence of one lonely child and the truth he represents destroy Connor's family? Or is it possible that healing and hope might come in the shape of a seven-year-old boy?

Softcover: 0-310-24749-7

Unabridged Audio Pages® CD: 0-310-25403-5

Pick up a copy today at your favorite bookstore!

GRAND RAPIDS, MICHIGAN 49530 USA

WWW.ZONDERVAN.COM

Cape Refuge

Terri Blackstock

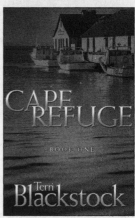

Mystery and suspense combine in this first book of an exciting new 4-book series by bestselling author Terri Blackstock.

Thelma and Wayne Owens run a bed and breakfast in Cape Refuge, Georgia. After a heated, public argument with his in-laws, Jonathan discovers Thelma and Wayne murdered in the warehouse where they held their church services. Considered the prime suspect, Jonathan is arrested. Grief-stricken, Morgan and Blair launch their own investigation to help Matthew Cade, the town's young police chief, find the real killer. Shady characters and a raft of suspects keep the plot twisting and the suspense building as we learn not only who murdered Thelma and Wayne, but also the secrets about their family's past and the true reason for Blair's disfigurement.

Softcover: 0-310-23592-8

Southern Storm

Terri Blackstock

The second book in the bestselling Cape Refuge suspense series.

Police Chief Cade disappears without a trace after accidentally hitting a man with his patrol car and killing him. While the rest of the police force looks for him and chases a series of clues that condemn Cade as a murderer, Blair Owens can't believe he is guilty of such a crime. Instead, she conducts her own search for the truth.

Softcover: 0-310-23593-6

River's Edge
Cape Refuge Series

Terri Blackstock

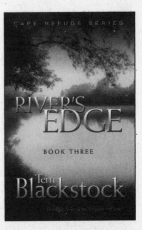

In Book Three of the #1 bestselling Cape
Refuge series, Terri Blackstock weaves
another riveting story of blackmail,
deceit, and murder. Reconciling themselves to the tragic death of her parents,
Morgan and Jonathan Cleary continue to
manage Hanover House, a residence for those seeking a new start
in life. They are also trying desperately to have a child. When
Jonathan is recruited to run for mayor, they are drawn into a
gritty campaign that tests their faith and ethics.

Ben Jackson seems to have the mayoral election locked up—
until his wife's body is found at the bottom of the river. Police
Chief Cade investigates Lisa's death and finds the facts of the
case don't add up. Lisa's best friend and partner is sure Ben is
responsible in some way. Rani Baxter claims Lisa had been
receiving mysterious letters written by a woman claiming she had
an affair with Ben. Even though Ben swore the letters were a
hoax, Blair Owens—in her new job as newspaper reporter—
begins searching for the woman who wrote the letters. Could
Lisa's death have anything to do with Ben's affair? Was it tied to
her decade-long quest to get pregnant? Does the fertility clinic
she'd been frequenting—the same one she encouraged Morgan
to visit—hold any clues? Was this an act of a jealous love? A dangerous client? Or is this all about the election?

Softcover: 0-310-23594-4

Brink of Death

Brandilyn Collins

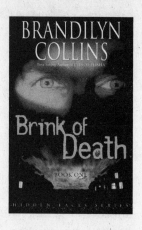

The noises, faint, fleeting, whispered into her consciousness like wraiths passing in the night.

Twelve-year-old Erin Willit opened her eyes to darkness lit only by the dim green nightlight near her closet door and the faint glow of a street lamp through her front window. She felt her forehead wrinkle, the fingers of one hand curl as she tried to discern what had awakened her.

Something was not right . . .

# # # #

Annie Kingston moves to Grove Landing for safety and quiet —and comes face to face with evil.

When neighbor Lisa Willet is killed by an intruder in her home, Sheriff's detectives are left with little evidence. Lisa's daughter, Erin, saw the killer, but she's too traumatized to give a description. The detectives grow desperate.

Because of her background in art, Annie is asked to question Erin and draw a composite. But Annie knows little about forensic art or the sensitive interview process. A nonbeliever, she finds herself begging God for help. What if her lack of experience leads Erin astray? The detectives could end up searching for a face that doesn't exist leaving the real killer free to stalk the neighborhood . . .

Softcover: 0-310-25103-6

GRAND RAPIDS, MICHIGAN 49530 USA

WWW.ZONDERVAN.COM

Eyes of Elisha

Brandilyn Collins

The murder was ugly.

The killer was sure no one saw him. Someone did.

In a horrifying vision, Chelsea Adams has relived the victim's last moments. But who will believe her? Certainly not the police, who must rely on hard evidence. Nor her husband, who barely tolerates Chelsea's newfound Christian faith. Besides, he's about to hire the man who Chelsea is certain is the killer to be a vice president in his company.

Torn between what she knows and the burden of proof, Chelsea must follow God's leading and trust him for protection. Meanwhile, the murderer is at liberty. And he's not about to take Chelsea's involvement lying down.

Softcover: 0-310-23968-0

Pick up a copy today at your favorite bookstore!

ZONDERVAN™

GRAND RAPIDS, MICHIGAN 49530 USA

WWW.ZONDERVAN.COM

Dread Champion

Brandilyn Collins

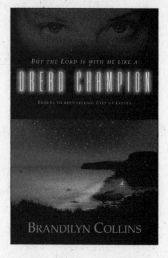

Chelsea Adams has visions. But they have no place in a courtroom. As a juror for a murder trial, Chelsea must rely only on the evidence. And this circumstantial evidence is strong —Darren Welk killed his wife. Or did he?

The trial is a nightmare for Chelsea. The other jurors belittle her Christian faith. As testimony unfolds, truth and secrets blur. Chelsea's visiting niece stumbles into peril surrounding the case, and Chelsea cannot protect her. God sends visions—frightening, vivid. But what do they mean? Even as Chelsea finds out, what can she do? She is helpless, and danger is closing in. . . .

Softcover: 0-310-23827-7

The Unthinkable Has Finally Happened. Can Chance Reynolds Face a Life without Racing?

Turn Four
A Novel of the Superspeedways

Tom Morrisey

Before he even had his driver's license, Chance Reynolds was racing—and winning. He worked his way up the racing ranks from go-carts to sprint cars to stock cars, exercising a natural talent that made him one of the best drivers in the Midwest. Now he has captured the points lead in stock-car racing's premiere series, and is a favorite to win the championship . . . until an off-track accident shatters his career and his life.

Riddled with doubts and questions, Chance delves into the Bible, looking for answers, a clear path for the next turn in his life. The thought of leaving the racing world is mind-numbing —it's all he has ever known.

Turn Four is an unforgettable ride through the realities of professional racing. Cloaked in the fanfare, it's a life of seeming comfort and glory. But underneath it all, people are searching for meaning in life, for love, for God.

Buckle up and hold on tight!

"Not only grabs a reader's attention; the book teaches all you need to know about the inner world of stock-car racing. This book will surprise you with a treasury of life lessons."
—Dale Beaver, Nextel Cup Chaplain, Motor Racing Outreach

Softcover: 0-310-23969-9

ZONDERVAN™

GRAND RAPIDS, MICHIGAN 49530 USA

WWW.ZONDERVAN.COM

Breach of Promise

James Scott Bell

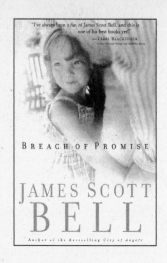

How far will a father go to get back his only daughter?

And how will he survive in a legal system that crushes those who can't afford to fight back?

Mark Gillen has the storybook life other men dream of, complete with a beautiful wife and an adoring five-year-old daughter.

Then his wife announces she's leaving him. And taking their daughter with her.

The other man is a famous film director with unlimited funds and the keys to stardom and wealth for Paula. How can Mark begin to compete? But the most bitter blow comes when he is kept from seeing his daughter because of false charges ... and a legal system ill-suited for finding the truth.

Forged in the darkest valley Mark has ever walked through, his faith in God may ultimately cost him everything in the eyes of the family law system. But it is the one thing that can keep him sane-and give him the strength to fight against all odds for what matters most.

Softcover: 0-310-24387-4

Pick up a copy today at your favorite bookstore!

ZONDERVAN™

GRAND RAPIDS, MICHIGAN 49530 USA

WWW.ZONDERVAN.COM

We want to hear from you. Please send your comments about this book to us in care of zreview@zondervan.com. Thank you.

GRAND RAPIDS, MICHIGAN 49530 USA

WWW.ZONDERVAN.COM